feeding baby

Joachim Splichal
& Christine Splichal

with PAMELA MOSHER

feeding

SIMPLE, HEALTHY RECIPES for BABIES and THEIR FAMILIES

BABY

Food photography by
VICTORIA PEARSON

Ten Speed Press
berkeley | toronto

🔟

Ten Speed Press

P.O. Box 7123

Berkeley, California 94707

www.tenspeed.com

Distributed in Australia by Simon & Schuster Australia, in Canada by Ten Speed Press Canada, in New Zealand by Southern Publishers Group, in South Africa by Real Books, and in the United Kingdom and Europe by Airlift Book Company.

Jacket and text design by Toni Tajima

Photos on pages 6, 34, 64, 71, 94, 108, 113, 135, and 139 by Sam Nicholson and Dianna Oliva Day. Photo on page 17 by Colleen Dunn Bates. Photos on pages 20 and 66 by Camille Renk. Photo on page 32 by Augustine Garza. Photos on pages 104 and 125 by Susan Goines.

Our thanks to Neiman Marcus Beverly Hills for providing props for photography. On page 41, ceramic plates by Christiane Perrochon exclusively for Neiman Marcus. On page 81, white dinner plate by Thierry Cheyron. On page 121, silver cup and silver baby fork by Reed & Barton and small pale gray plate by Christiane Perrochon. On page 127, bib by Neiman Marcus.

Library of Congress Cataloging-in-Publication Data

Splichal, Joachim.

    Feeding Baby : simple healthy recipes for babies and their families / Joachim Splichal and Christine Splichal.

        p. cm.

    Includes bibliographical references and index.

    ISBN 1-58008-500-8

    1. Infants (Newborn)—Nutrition. 2. Infants—Nutrition. 3. Toddlers—Nutrition. 4. Cookery (Baby foods) I. Splichal, Christine. II. Title.

                                  RJ216.S657 2003

613.2'083'2—dc21

Printed in China

First printing, 2003

1 2 3 4 5 6 7 8 9 10 — 07 06 05 04 03

For our twins, Nicolas and Stephane,
who inspired us to rediscover the pleasures of
honest, simple foods.

contents

Acknowledgments | viii

Introduction | 1

Getting Started | 7

1 **Tastes** *Six to Nine Months* | 13

2 **Nibbles** *Nine to Twelve Months* | 25

3 **Bites** *One to Two Years* | 47

4 **Meals** *Two to Three Years* | 65

5 **Family Feasts** | 94

Recommended Reading | 154

Metric Conversions | 156

Index | 157

acknowledgments

We would like to thank the dedicated and talented crew that brought this book to completion. Our gratitude goes to Kristy Melville, publisher at Ten Speed Press, who enthusiastically embraced the project; editor Carrie Rodrigues, who shepherded the book to press with a discerning eye; Brigit Binns, who consulted with us early on in the project and got us focused; Camille Renk, who thoroughly tested the recipes; Pamela Mosher, who worked with us to write the recipes and recount our experiences; pediatric dietitian Gail Seche, whose expertise was invaluable; photographer Victoria Pearson, who can turn a dish of carrot purée into a candidate for the cover of Gourmet (and probably has done so at some point); stylist Ann Johnstad, who seems to know intuitively how objects can tell stories; and designer Toni Tajima, who brought it all so brilliantly to the page. And we are very grateful to Sam Nicholson and Diana Oliva Day for their wonderful, candid photos of our family and Maria and Augustine Garza, Camille and Bernhard Renk, Susan and Octavio Becerra, and Darryl and Colleen Dunn Bates, who contributed photos of their own adorable offspring.

introduction

When our twins were born, people often asked us how we managed to find the time to start our babies off eating freshly prepared food instead of conventional bottled baby food. The truth is that it wasn't a huge ordeal for us; it was simply a natural progression because of who we are and the role food plays in our lives. We started giving our boys "real" food—purées and mashed, steamed vegetables—at about four months. By the time they were eleven months old, we'd all have something like sweet potato risotto, pink lentils with peaches, or Napa cabbage with lemon and bacon for dinner. We adults might add a piece of fish or meat to round out our own menu, but everyone sat at the same table and ate the same food together—simple, fresh, honest, and, above all, nutritious food. Just because we run "gourmet" restaurants doesn't mean we feed our kids "gourmet" food. If they want to eat gourmet food, that's something they can decide later.

This is not a revolutionary concept. In fact, it's quite old-fashioned. Before the industrialization of food preparation, everyone had to make meals from scratch for their babies. The advent of canning and bottling was a quantum leap forward, and when bottled baby food became available, it must have seemed like modern, time-saving progress at its best. Because we are creatures of habit, the common approach for many years now has been to just "go with the flow" and serve baby bottled food. But we feel something important has been lost. It's not just the vitamins and minerals that are destroyed when fresh food is bottled and heat-treated to improve shelf life, it's the warm feeling that comes from sitting around the table and "breaking bread" together as a family. We believe that the practice of feeding baby processed food has contributed to the practice of eating different foods at different times of the day, even when the children are older. Surely this is not good for the nuclear family.

There is a tendency in these busy times to rely on prepared foods for meals. Just take a stroll through a supermarket and see how many baskets are full of packaged, premade meals, and how few fresh vegetables are in those same baskets. Real food is a wonderful thing! The crunch of a fresh carrot, the briny smell of a freshly caught fish, the snap of crisp green beans . . . we have a responsibility to our children to promote the practice of eating real, fresh food, prepared the old-fashioned way, with our hands. If we can familiarize our children now with the tastes and textures of real food as opposed to processed, prepared food, then we are sending them on a healthy, happy road to adulthood and all the myriad pleasures of food. And it's important to remember that food comes from the earth, not from a plastic box or bag. There's nothing wrong with seeing a little dirt on our food, and that's why we love the farmers' markets springing up all over the country. They're good for the consumers and good for the farmers. Let's make sure these markets and the choice of fresh vegetables in our supermarkets remain available until our children grow up. We're all aware of the importance of fresh food, and we doubt that most adults would want to live on a diet of canned foods. So why should we expect it of our children?

Our kids are seven years old now, and it's very gratifying for us as parents to see the results of our endeavors. An example we saw very early on was during the holiday season several years ago. At Christmas the kids had exactly what we had—not the whole multicourse meal, of course, but one or two parts of it. Nicolas even said to the cook, "Very good, très bon!" He was two and a half! We were proud parents. We went to visit friends for Thanksgiving and the other kids at the table refused to eat most of the food, but our boys were game for everything. All we had to do was cut it up.

We can now give them just about any food, and 99 percent of the time they have what we're having. They aren't likely to turn their noses up at foods that aren't familiar, because almost everything is familiar. For instance, for lunch we might all have braised pork with apricots and onions—we just cut theirs up and have ours whole. The next day we might have lamb stew with carrots and prunes, or tuna with roasted garlic and tomatoes. It's all fresh, healthy food, and it's not scary to the kids. Of course, there are exceptions. For some reason, they don't like Brussels sprouts. But we know many adults who don't like Brussels sprouts, either. In writing this book, we are hoping to share our strategies, trials, and successes with a wider audience.

Of course, everyone wants the very best for their babies, there's no question about that. But we're all busy people, and most of us don't have help at home. Preparing food from scratch for baby might, at first, sound like a lot of trouble. Far from it! If you have a steamer basket, almost any vegetable can be steamed in 3 to 8 minutes (after the water boils). For the first few months after breast-feeding stops, you'll have to throw it in the blender, but after that you'll only have to chop it up a little. After a few months of puréeing, the kids can eat exactly what the rest of the family eats, with a few exceptions. Instead of being more trouble, it's actually less. If the grown-ups are having lamb chops for supper, make up a batch of white beans with parsley and garlic. For the kids it makes a healthy main course, for you a tasty side dish. There is also a cost benefit. Bottled baby foods are expensive, and often the full bottle doesn't get used. Sharing the same food among the whole family means less expense and less waste.

Most importantly, it's healthy food. Kids, not just here in the States but in other parts of the world as well, tend to eat unhealthy food. They start out with bland, soft food and then don't want to explore beyond those flavors and textures. How many times have you heard kids yelling for pizza instead of what the adults are having? And it's not even real pizza! It's bland topping on soft dough with too much cheese, washed down with sugary soda. They develop bad habits and continue them into adolescence and young adulthood, often resulting in problems with obesity and poor health. We decided early on that sweetened sodas never would be found in our refrigerator. They are full of sugar, and a sure recipe for dental problems. Fruit juice and water are the only beverages on the menu.

If you make your children aware from an early age that there is something else besides bland, fatty fast food, they will develop a palate and always be open to new tastes. And another important point: when it comes to vitamins and nutrients, there is simply no comparison between bottled food and freshly made food. Prepared baby foods and juices can be full of sugar and preservatives. By making your own baby food, you'll know exactly what is going into it. This was a huge motivation for us in starting our kids off on fresh food, and we believe it will be a strong motivation for many other parents as well.

There is, of course, a science to the practice of good nutrition. That's why we have pediatric dietician Gail Seche helping us to make this book nutritionally sound. When we began this project, we read lots of books on nutrition. Christine basically gave herself a miniature course on the subject. Also, her father is extremely involved with naturopathy in France, and we had his advice, too. If you do some research and arm yourself with some of the wonderful books available, you'll be able to make informed decisions about what to feed your baby, and when.

Cautionary Advice

It is extremely important that, from the moment your baby begins to eat solids, her meals are always supervised. In addition to the bonding that takes place between baby and parent during feeding, it is important to watch for signs of allergic reaction and choking. The former will be of immediate concern, since the possibility of allergic reaction exists from the moment your baby ingests her first food other than breast milk. Choking, although always a concern, is more apt to occur when your baby progresses to food that is more chewy and textured. Since both an allergic reaction and choking require immediate response, your full attention should be focused on your baby during her meals.

ALLERGIES

As you make the transition from breast-feeding to feeding your baby solids, you may find that your baby will have an allergic reaction to certain foods. An allergic reaction is caused by the immune system's reaction to what it perceives as a threat. When an ingested food is identified as a foreign body, the immune system overproduces antibodies to counteract it.

Signs of allergic reaction vary from hives, which are usually immediate, to diarrhea, nausea, vomiting, difficulty breathing, runny nose, swelling of the lips or face, itching, and shock. Symptoms can appear from within minutes to up to two hours. Watch your baby carefully, since it's easy to read an allergic reaction as a cold or other illness. Consult your pediatrician to verify any suspicions.

Theories vary widely on what causes allergies, but if there is a history of food allergies in your family, there is a chance that your baby will develop similar ones. Those chances are increased if both parents have food allergies. Neither of us have food allergies, and, fortunately, our boys never developed any, but we were definitely on the watch for allergic reactions.

Good basic means of allergy prevention are breast-feeding and delaying the introduction of solids until your baby is at least six months old.

The generally accepted method to determine what foods cause an allergic reaction is called the four-day wait rule. Allergic reactions are not always immediate; it can be several days before a reaction occurs. For this reason, it's advisable to wait approximately four days after introducing a new food to see if an allergic reaction is triggered. Introduce the new food by itself, not mixed with anything else, in order to gauge its effect. During the waiting period, previously tested foods can be served but do not introduce any other new foods. Don't overdo it with the new food because too frequent feedings of a new food can create a sensitivity to it.

Known allergens are the ones to watch, especially if there is a family history. Among these are cow's milk, soy, egg white, wheat, peanuts and possibly other nuts, shellfish, pork, corn, and strawberries. Some allergies will decline as your baby gets older, and some, especially allergies to eggs, cow's milk, wheat, and shellfish, will remain throughout life.

In the case of cow's milk, a distinction should be made between an allergic reaction and lactose intolerance, which doesn't involve the immune system. Lactase is the enzyme that breaks down milk sugar, lactose, in the intestines. If your baby's intestines lack the enzyme, the lactose is not digested and bacteria develop, causing gas, abdominal pain, and diarrhea. Symptoms can occur within thirty minutes to up to two hours.

CHOKING

In general, the risk of choking is greatest for children under three years of age, although older children are susceptible as well. Small, hard objects are usually the culprits. Among these are popcorn, berries, raisins, nut pieces, hard candy, seeds, and hard pieces of fruit or vegetables—in short, anything that is hard, small enough to fit in your child's mouth, and large enough to become lodged in his throat or windpipe.

In addition to being watchful, you can take other precautions. Cut up the food into pieces small enough that they can be swallowed and not lodge in your child's throat. Never let your child eat while he is lying down or walking around. Make sure that breads or biscuits, such as teething biscuits, are either too hard for a piece to break off or soft enough to dissolve when put into your child's mouth.

You'll know your child is choking if she has difficulty breathing, her arms are flailing, she can't cough up the blockage, or she is starting to turn blue. Be extremely cautious about trying to manually remove the stuck object; you could push it in further and worsen the situation. Call for emergency medical help immediately. If you are not already trained in CPR, it is a good idea to take one of the classes offered by your local Red Cross chapter or hospital.

A WORD ABOUT SALT

Resist adding salt to your baby's food until they are over two years old. Your baby will easily get the required daily amount of sodium from his normal diet. Since many of the recipes in the book are also intended for adults, they contain salt. The majority of these are in the Meals chapter, for children two to three years old, and Family Feasts, for the entire family. However, salt can be eliminated or reduced when preparing any of these recipes for your baby. Since she hasn't developed a taste for salt, she won't find the food prepared from these recipes bland. Conversely, many of the recipes for children younger than two are also suitable for older children and adults. Salt can be added to make these recipes palatable for them.

How to Use This Book

The recipes offered here are adaptable. Some are intended for babies and some for grown-ups, but we like to think they'll be used for both because that's the way we do it at our house. You won't feed baby everything you eat, but baby's food easily can play a big role in your own menu. In fact, you'll probably eat more nutritious food than usual if you eat the same food you prepare for baby. In the summer, make Salmon with Couscous and Roasted Green Onions (page 40) for baby's lunch—but make enough so it's a ready-made dinner for the rest of the family. The result: Baby has had protein for lunch, and you have made yourself an easy, delicious dinner.

Or, steam some broccoli and cauliflower, then toss half or three-quarters of it with some salad greens and vinaigrette for your own lunch. Save the rest for baby's dinner, and all that's left to do is chop and serve. The combinations are endless, and your own creativity is bound to come into play. The best part is that you and your baby are both eating fresh, flavorful food full of vitamins and minerals and without added sugar or preservatives. Plus, you are nurturing a young soul toward a lifetime of adventurous, healthy eating and civilized dining.

getting started

t he first step when approaching a new recipe is to read it all the way through before you begin. This will enable you to assemble the necessary ingredients so that they are ready for use. You can also devise your strategy, especially if you are preparing a meal with several dishes or courses.

Basic Techniques

The recipes in this book do not reflect the haute cuisine that I am known for at Patina, but many of the techniques are identical to those used in the restaurant's kitchen, and they are simple. Blanching and refreshing are standard procedures for preparing green vegetables and some fruits, whether I'm cooking at the restaurant or in my kitchen. Braising is a traditional method that makes the most of a large piece of meat, and deglazing is essential to create the delicious sauce. A very useful technique to master, caramelizing adds a delicate sweet, slightly burnt flavor to onions, apples, and most famously crème brûlée and crème caramel. Freezing and reheating are simple, logical procedures that you will become an expert at during your first months of parenthood.

BLANCHING AND REFRESHING

Blanching preserves the flavor, texture, and color of vegetables, and some fruits, and prepares them for further cooking. Fill a large bowl with ice water. Bring to a boil a pot of water that is large enough for the amount of vegetables being prepared. Drop the vegetables gently into the pot and cook, uncovered, until they're brightly colored, usually 2 to 3 minutes, or whatever is recommended in the recipe. Remove them immediately with a slotted spoon and plunge into the bowl of ice water, which stops the cooking. This practice is also known as refreshing the vegetables. Once drained, the vegetables are ready to be sautéed, puréed, or, in the case of tomatoes or thin-skinned fruit, peeled.

BRAISING

Braising is a wonderful method of preparing large cuts of meat, usually pot roasts or veal shanks, that produces tender, flavorful results. Heat olive oil in a large Dutch oven, sear the meat on all sides, season with salt and pepper, add vegetables and stock—whatever the recipe calls for—and then cover tightly and place in the oven or leave on the stovetop over low heat to simmer, according to the recipe. A delicious crust will form on the meat, and it will be so tender it will almost fall off the bone, if there is a bone involved.

CARAMELIZING

Sugar is the principal agent in the caramelizing process. Sugar is dissolved in water and heated, as the pan is swirled, until it turns into a golden brown—or caramel—colored syrup. Apples and onions can be caramelized by sprinkling them with sugar and sautéing them in butter or oil until a golden brown glaze forms.

DEGLAZING

Deglazing is generally the first step to preparing a sauce. To a pan in which meat has been seared, add liquid—veal stock, wine, cream, lemon juice, or vegetable broth—and heat while scraping up the browned bits of meat with a wooden spoon. Continue cooking and stirring until the liquid is reduced and thickened, or use the liquid as the base for a sauce.

FREEZING, THAWING, AND REHEATING BABY FOOD

Most of the foods that you prepare for your baby can be safely stored in the refrigerator, covered tightly, for 1 day. It is best to use a heatproof microwave dish that you can either pop in the microwave or set in a small pan partially filled with boiling water to heat. Tepid food is a breeding ground for bacteria, so always reheat the food until it is hot—about 165°F for 2 minutes—and don't reheat it more than once. Stir it thoroughly and taste it before serving to make sure it's cool enough.

If the food won't be eaten the next day, freeze it for later. Although we are not advocates of frozen food in general, freezing baby food, especially purées, is extremely practical and ensures that there is always good homemade food available. Your baby's consumption of those first solids will be very small, so you will always have more food than is required, unless you eat the rest yourself, which may be tempting. Place leftovers in a plastic ice cube tray, cover it tightly with aluminum foil, and freeze it. When frozen solid, remove the cubes and place them in a freezer bag for later use. Mark the date and contents on the bag.

Ice cube trays aren't the only choice for freezing. Less liquid food can be placed in scoops or blobs on a tray or dish, covered with foil, and frozen. As with the ice cubes, once frozen solid, the blobs can be sealed in a freezer bag, dated, and stored.

Although it depends on the type, almost all frozen foods will keep for at least 2 months. Either thaw the frozen food overnight in the refrigerator or slowly heat it in a pan on the stove, stirring just until it is warm. Always taste the food to make sure that it is completely thawed and not too hot. Microwaves can be used—according to the defrost mode instructions—but you must make sure that the food is thoroughly stirred to eliminate hot and cold spots.

Never refreeze thawed food or baby food made with frozen vegetables or other frozen foods. It is a health hazard.

Necessary Equipment

Cooking in my restaurant, Patina, and cooking at home present two vastly different scenarios. At the restaurant, I have legions of prep cooks to assemble my mise en place—the ingredients—all nicely chopped, shredded, peeled, sliced, or whatever is required to be prepared to the point of cooking. At home, since neither my wife nor I have much time, we rely for prepping on some handy appliances and the usual batterie du cuisine, that is, kitchen equipment.

You probably already have most of the equipment necessary to prepare the recipes in this book, but the following items are indispensable.

BLENDER

A blender will be your most useful appliance once you start your baby on solid food. It produces a finer purée than a food processor and can truly liquefy food. A blender accessory, the mini-blend bowl, is very useful for blending small amounts of food and grinding cheese, nuts, and porridge.

STICK BLENDER

A luxury, but a handy one, is the stick blender. In the mixing beaker that it comes with, you can quickly purée, blend, or whisk small portions of food. You can also use it right in saucepans on the stove or in serving bowls and avoid having more dishes to wash.

FOOD PROCESSOR

The food processor is the all-around most useful appliance you can own. It chops, slices, mixes, and purées everything from vegetables to meat to egg whites and bread. The pulse feature, which redistributes the food each time it is pressed, allows you to finely control the degree of processing. They come in a variety of sizes, from 3 to 4 cups, to up to 14. Get the largest one that suits your needs and your budget. You'll find that as you become familiar with its features, you'll be using it constantly. You'll want to make sure you have room for it on your counter and possibly under your cupboards.

STAND MIXER

The stand mixer, with its variety of useful attachments, can mix bread dough, beat egg whites into snowy peaks, cream butter, and even grind meat, with little human interaction, since the head moves in a circular fashion from the edge to the center of the bowl, thoroughly mixing the contents. Especially popular with serious home bakers, stand mixers come in several capacities and horsepowers. Choose one based on your budget and requirements.

HAND MIXER

Once the principle piece of equipment in most kitchens, the hand mixer has taken a back seat to its more capable successors, the food processor and the stand mixer. It still has its uses, however. Light, compact, and mobile, it can mix relatively small amounts at a choice of several speeds.

STEAMERS

Steamers come in a variety of materials and styles from the simple, collapsible metal insert to the traditional Asian bamboo steamer to a three-tiered stainless steel model. Steaming not only retains nutrients but—in the two- and three-tiered steamers—allows for several components of a meal to be cooked at once. Christine's dad, a naturopathy enthusiast, is a firm believer in steaming.

STRAINERS AND SIEVES

Both implements separate liquid from solids but do so to different degrees. Strainers usually have a coarser mesh or holes, such as a colander; sieves, with their finer mesh, are also used for dry ingredients, such as flour, confectioners' sugar, and powders. Sieves are available in a variety of sizes and materials. There is the large, flat-bottomed drum sieve, for large amounts, the cup-size flour sifter with a trigger handle, and the chinois, a conical sieve with a shaped-to-fit wooden pestle that extracts every last drop from cooked vegetables and other mixtures. Sieves can be used to smooth out gravies and remove seeds from raspberries. Until your baby is six months old, you'll be using a sieve constantly to make sure there are no fruit seeds or lumps in the purées.

POTATO RICER

The potato ricer banishes lumps from mashed potatoes, other cooked root vegetables, and firm-fleshed fruit, such as apples. When pressed through the ricer, boiled potato emerges in soft rice-size bits. The ricer can be found in either metal or plastic models and some have interchangeable screens with a range of hole sizes.

WOODEN SPOONS

The most obvious advantage of a wooden spoon is that it doesn't conduct heat. It feels good in the hand and is the preferred utensil for stirring risotto, making gravy, and deglazing a pan. Look for spoons made of boxwood or beech, which won't react with food and won't easily splinter or crack.

DUTCH OVEN

A cast-iron round or oval pot with small handles on either side, the Dutch oven is the pot to use for braising and stews. It can go from the stovetop into the oven and, if attractively clad in enamel, can be placed on the table for serving. It has a flat, thick base for browning and evenly distributing heat, and can hold from 2 to 13 quarts.

ICE CUBE TRAYS

Ice trays are perfect for freezing purées or soups in convenient sizes. Large, flexible plastic or rubber trays are best, making it easy to remove individual cubes.

PARCHMENT PAPER

Impervious to grease and moisture, parchment paper is used to line baking pans.

1 Tastes

six to nine months

With our boys, we made the transition from breast-feeding to "solids" when they were four to five months old. That may feel too soon for many parents, which is why we have started the recipes at six months. By then vegetable and grain purées are usually being introduced into the baby's diet.

Between four and six months, your baby's digestive system will be developed enough to handle solid foods. Indications that your baby is ready are that she has doubled her birth weight and weighs at least thirteen to fifteen pounds; she's able to sit up with support and hold her head up; time between feedings decreases or she refuses the breast; and she stops thrusting her tongue out when you attempt to put a spoon in her mouth. Your baby may also begin to show interest in others eating and may attempt to feed herself. Your pediatrician, however, is the final authority on when to start your baby on solid food.

roasted acorn squash purée | 14

carrot with chicken broth purée | 16

fresh pea with mint purée | 17

couscous with corn and pea purée | 18

green beans and wax beans | 19

green or brown lentil with carrot and shallot purée | 20

pink lentil and peach purée | 21

rosemary breadsticks | 22

roasted acorn squash purée

Squash is rich in beta-carotene, folic acid, and fiber, making it a good choice for your baby's diet. The brown sugar and cinnamon are optional, although they add a wonderful flavor to the squash and will make it enticing for older children and adults.

NOTES

The squash can be prepared to the point before the chicken broth is added and kept in the refrigerator for up to two days. To finish, purée with the warmed chicken broth. Leftover purée can be frozen or mixed into yogurt or a soup.

Makes 3 cups

2 acorn squash, about
   5 inches in diameter,
   halved and seeds and
   strings removed

3 tablespoons extra virgin
   olive oil

¼ cup firmly packed dark
   brown sugar (optional)

¼ teaspoon ground
   cinnamon (optional)

2 tablespoons low-sodium
   chicken broth, warmed

1. Preheat the oven to 400°F.

2. Set the squash halves cut side up, brush them with the oil, and sprinkle with the brown sugar and cinnamon. Wrap the halves in aluminum foil, place on a baking sheet, and roast for 30 to 40 minutes, until tender and easily pierced with the tip of a knife. Remove from the oven and set aside until cool enough to handle.

3. Scrape the flesh of the squash from the peel and transfer to a blender or food processor fitted with a steel blade. Add the warmed chicken broth and purée.

4. Serve immediately. Freeze leftover purée that won't be eaten the next day (see page 8).

carrot with chicken broth purée

By eight to nine months, babies are ready for foods with a thicker texture than purées. At that point, depending on your baby's ability to chew, you can mash the carrot pieces instead of puréeing them.

Makes 2 cups

2 cups low-sodium chicken broth

1 pound carrots, peeled and cut into ¼-inch rounds

2 teaspoons unsalted butter, at room temperature

1. In a medium saucepan over high heat, bring the broth to a boil.

2. Add the carrots and cook for 10 to 12 minutes, until the carrots are tender and easily pierced with the tip of a knife. Remove the pan from the heat. Remove the carrots from the broth with a slotted spoon, reserving the liquid.

3. Combine the carrots and butter in a blender and purée, adding the reserved broth until the mixture is creamy.

4. Serve warm. Freeze leftover purée that won't be eaten the next day (see page 8).

SCHEDULED MEAL TIMES

There are two definite schools of thought on whether or not to feed babies according to a schedule. Being both a new mother and an older mother, I was very serious and did a lot of research on the subject. One book that influenced me was from France, written by a woman with a very Germanic style who had cared for hundreds of babies and was very adamant about the necessity of a set feeding schedule, especially for twins. I followed her advice with very satisfactory results, otherwise I would have been feeding them constantly. For the first three months, they were on a strict schedule, which made everything easier, including the introduction of solid food.   —C.S.

fresh pea with mint purée

Peas were an early favorite with our kids because of their naturally sweet flavor. They also liked to throw them.

Makes 1 cup

2 cups freshly shelled peas

1 carrot, peeled and diced

1 celery stalk, trimmed and cut into small pieces

1 tablespoon unsalted butter, at room temperature

⅛ teaspoon minced fresh mint (optional)

1. Bring a large saucepan of water to a boil. Add the peas, carrot, and celery and cook for about 2 minutes, until the peas are bright green and tender. Remove from the heat and drain, reserving some liquid for puréeing. Refresh the vegetables in ice water and drain.

2. In a blender or food processor fitted with a steel blade, combine the vegetables with the butter and mint, and pulse until smooth, adding the reserved liquid as necessary to achieve the desired consistency.

3. Serve immediately. Freeze leftover purée that won't be eaten the next day (see page 8).

couscous with corn and pea purée

We treat couscous as if it were a grain, when in fact it is tiny pasta. If time is critical, frozen peas and corn kernels can be used in this dish. The flavor and nutritional value, however, are always better with fresh.

Makes 3 cups

1 cup corn kernels, freshly scraped from the cob

1 cup freshly shelled peas

2 cups water

1⅓ cups couscous

2 tablespoons unsalted butter

1. Bring a medium saucepan halfway filled with water to a boil. Add the corn and boil for about 2 minutes, until the corn is tender. Remove the kernels with a slotted spoon and set aside.

2. Add the peas to the same boiling water and boil for 2 minutes, until the peas are bright green and tender. Drain and refresh the peas in ice water. When cool, drain and set aside.

3. In a large saucepan, bring the 2 cups water to a boil. Add the couscous and the butter, stir, and cover. Decrease the heat to a simmer and cook for about 2 minutes.

4. Add the corn and peas to the couscous, remove from the heat, and let stand for about 5 minutes. Transfer to a blender or food processor fitted with a steel blade and pulse until smooth.

5. Serve immediately. Freeze leftover purée that won't be eaten the next day (see page 8). (If you have used frozen vegetables to make this, don't freeze the leftovers. Frozen food should never be refrozen after it has been thawed.)

THE INGREDIENTS WE USE

In the lists of ingredients for the recipes, you'll see extra virgin olive oil, sea salt, and organic fruits and poultry. Although these recipes can be prepared with regular salt and olive oil, and produce that is not organic, we want to recommend what we feel is the best—best for taste and best for health.   —C.S.

green beans and wax beans

At about seven months, your baby will be ready for green and wax beans. For older babies and uncivilized adults, green beans make great finger food.

NOTES ▶ **Mash or purée the beans until your baby is nine months old.**

Makes 3 cups

¼ **pound green beans, trimmed**

¼ **pound wax beans, trimmed**

3 **tablespoons unsalted butter**

¼ **teaspoon minced garlic**

1. In a large saucepan, bring a generous amount of water to a boil. Add the green beans to the boiling water and cook for 2 to 8 minutes until bright green and tender, depending on the freshness of the beans. Remove the beans with a slotted spoon and refresh in ice water. Drain.

2. Bring the water back to a boil. Add the wax beans and cook for 2 to 8 minutes, depending on the freshness of the beans. Drain. Refresh the beans in ice water, then drain.

3. Heat the butter in a large sauté pan over medium-high heat. Add the garlic and cook for 2 minutes. Add the beans and sauté for about 3 minutes until warm, stirring to coat them evenly with the butter and garlic.

4. Serve immediately, if you are serving the beans whole. To purée, roughly chop and combine the beans in a blender with as much water as necessary to reach the desired consistency, about 1 cup. Freeze leftovers that won't be eaten the next day (see page 8).

green or brown lentil with carrot and shallot purée

Brown lentils cook a little quicker than the smaller green French or Le Puy lentils, which have a better flavor, and which we prefer. We served this dish to our kids once or twice a week.

NOTES ▶ **Onions can be substituted for shallots. Omit the onions for babies younger than nine months.**

Makes about 3 cups

4 cups low-sodium chicken broth

2 cups lentils, rinsed and picked over

2 carrots, peeled and finely chopped

1 teaspoon minced shallot or onion (optional)

1. In a large saucepan, combine the broth and lentils and bring to a boil. Add the carrots and shallot. Decrease the heat to a simmer and cook for about 30 minutes, until the lentils and vegetables are tender. Drain and reserve the liquid.

2. Transfer the lentil mixture to a blender and pulse until smooth, slowly adding the reserved cooking liquid.

3. Serve immediately. Freeze leftover purée that won't be eaten the next day (see page 8).

pink lentil and peach purée

We like lentils and we like peaches. The two complement each other on the palate and, for an adult version, visually. This makes a good savory-sweet side dish.

NOTES ▶ **Double the ingredients to make four adult servings, and don't purée, of course. Pink lentils are sometimes referred to as red. Either can be used.**

Makes 1 cup

2 fresh peaches, peeled, halved, and pitted

¼ cup minced onion

3 tablespoons unsalted butter

2½ cups low-sodium chicken broth, plus extra for purée, warmed

½ cup pink lentils, rinsed and picked over

1 teaspoon red wine vinegar

1. Preheat the oven to 350°F. Line a baking sheet with parchment paper.

2. Place the peach halves cut side up on the baking sheet and bake for about 30 minutes, until tender. When cool, cut the peaches into ½-inch dice.

3. In a medium saucepan, sauté the onion in the butter for about 3 minutes, until it softens. Add the 2½ cups broth and bring to a boil over medium-high heat. Add the lentils and vinegar, and cook 10 to 15 minutes, until most of the liquid has been absorbed. Add the peaches and cook for 1 to 2 minutes more.

4. Combine the lentil mixture in a blender or food processor fitted with a steel blade with about ¼ cup warm broth and purée.

5. Serve warm or at room temperature. Freeze leftover purée that won't be eaten the next day (see page 8).

rosemary bread sticks

Give these bread sticks an authentic Italian touch by flavoring them with rosemary leaves preserved in salt. This is easily prepared by sealing ¼ cup rosemary leaves with an equal amount of sea salt in a jar with a lid. Let it sit for three days before use.

> **NOTES** **Salt can be reduced or eliminated from the recipe for children younger than two years old.**

Makes 28 bread sticks

STARTER

1 package (2½ teaspoons)
    active dry yeast

1½ cups warm water

½ teaspoon sea salt
    (optional)

2 cups plus 1 tablespoon
    all-purpose flour

BREAD STICK DOUGH

¼ cup extra virgin olive oil

¼ cup fresh rosemary leaves,
    finely chopped

Sea salt and freshly ground
    black pepper

2½ cups all-purpose flour

1. To make the starter, in the bowl of a stand mixer, dissolve the yeast in the water, and let it sit for 10 minutes. Add the salt and the 2 cups flour. Using the hook attachment, mix at low speed, gradually increasing to high until smooth.

2. Transfer the starter to a bowl and sprinkle with the 1 tablespoon flour. Cover the bowl with plastic wrap or a damp dishtowel and set it in a warm, draft-free spot for about 1 hour, until the starter has doubled in size. (The starter has doubled in size when the table-spoon of flour is no longer visible or large cracks appear on top.)

3. To make the dough, transfer the starter to the bowl of the stand mixer with the hook attachment. Add the oil, rosemary, salt and pepper, and mix well on low. With the mixer on low speed, add the flour in ½-cup increments. Repeat until 2 cups of flour have been added and the dough forms into a sticky ball.

4. Preheat the oven to 400°F. Grease a sheet pan very lightly with olive oil.

5. Turn the dough out onto a lightly floured surface. Sprinkle it with the remaining ½ cup of flour, and knead by hand for about 10 minutes, until the dough is smooth and elastic.

6. Take a 1-ounce portion of dough and roll it on the work surface with both hands in a back-and-forth motion, moving your hands outward as the stick takes shape. Sprinkle it with flour only if the dough sticks to the work surface. Roll out to 16 to 18 inches in length and ¼ inch in diameter. The sticks needn't be identical; the charm is their hand-rolled appearance.

7. Lay the sticks on the baking sheet. Bake 5 to 8 minutes, until crisp and brown. Remove the bread sticks from the oven and let cool.

8. Serve as a snack or with a meal.

THE TRANSITION TO SOLIDS

In Europe we tend to start babies on solids a little earlier than in the United States.

We began feeding the boys puréed foods at around four to five months. I avoided rice cereal, which is a standard here, I believe, because I didn't want them to develop a taste for plain starch. Steamed and puréed carrots, sweet potatoes with a bit of butter, and mashed bananas were their first real foods. We progressed rapidly from mild foods to puréed leeks and watercress with homemade applesauce, and fish.

Many new mothers express concern over butter, but babies need fat in their diets; any child nutritionist will tell you that. Babies' bodies are busy forming bones and muscles, and that can't happen without some dietary fat.

By about eight months old, the boys were eating exactly what we were eating, with a few exceptions. We served them lots of vegetables, accompanied by meat or fish usually only at lunch, allowing plenty of time for them to digest before they went to bed for the night. We prefer the European tradition of making lunch the day's main meal and dinner very light. Afternoon snacks consisted of a little apple juice, mandarin orange segments, maybe some papaya, and, very rarely, a cookie. For dinner, it was usually grains or cereals, like couscous with cauliflower and carrots, or brown rice with ground roasted hazelnuts and apples.   —C.S.

2 Nibbles

nine to twelve months

around nine months, we began adding meat, poultry, and fish to the boys' meals. In fact, we often just minced up a little of what we were eating. The texture of the food can be chunkier as babies learn to chew. Many of the purées from the previous chapter can be simply mashed for babies in this age group.

Serving sizes, other than for purées, are for two adults and two to four children, depending on the ages of the children and whether the dish will be served as a main course or side dish for adults.

sautéed broccoli purée | 26

broccoli and cauliflower purée | 27

carrot purée with lemon | 28

celery root and fresh basil purée | 30

parsnips, apples, and sweet onions | 31

potato and leek purée | 32

creamed spinach | 33

fresh sweet peas and ham | 34

turnips, pears, and parsley | 35

black beans and banana with créme fraîche | 37

couscous with cauliflower and carrots | 39

salmon with couscous and roasted green onions | 40

focaccia | 42

sweet potato risotto | 43

banana peach compote | 44

sautéed broccoli purée

Sautéing the broccoli in butter adds an attractive nutty flavor to this dish.

Makes 3 cups

1 pound broccoli, florets cut into small pieces

3 tablespoons unsalted butter

½ cup whole milk

¼ cup low-sodium chicken broth, plus extra for puréeing, warmed

1. In a medium saucepan with a steamer, bring 2 inches of water to a boil.

2. Add the broccoli to the steamer, cover, and steam for 3 to 5 minutes until the broccoli is bright green and tender. Drain the broccoli and refresh in ice water. When cool, remove the broccoli from the water, drain, and set aside.

3. In a large sauté pan, heat the butter over medium heat until it begins to brown. Add the broccoli and sauté for 1 minute. Stir in the milk and the ¼ cup broth and cook for about 1 minute more, until the broccoli is lightly browned and heated through. Remove the pan from the heat and set aside to cool for 5 minutes.

4. Transfer the broccoli mixture to a blender and purée. Add more broth to achieve the desired consistency.

5. Serve at room temperature. Freeze leftover purée that won't be eaten the next day (see page 8).

RITUALS

Nicolas and Stephane have been brought up with a lifestyle very focused on food, which was how I was brought up. You invest time and interest in what you eat, which means time spent shopping and cooking. When the boys were six months old, we would take them with us to the farmers' market. They learned very early what vegetables look like before they're cooked and that all food doesn't come from the supermarket.   —C.S.

broccoli and cauliflower purée

Since both these vegetables are excellent sources of vitamin C and other nutrients, you should try to make them a staple of your baby's diet before he or she develops any ideas on the subject.

Makes 2 cups

½ **pound broccoli florets, cut into 3-inch pieces**

½ **pound cauliflower florets, cut into 3-inch pieces, core trimmed away**

¼ **cup unsalted butter**

½ **cup low-sodium chicken broth, plus extra for puréeing, warmed**

1. In a medium saucepan with a steamer, bring 2 inches of water to a boil.

2. Add the broccoli to the steamer, cover, and steam for 3 to 5 minutes until the broccoli is bright green and tender. When done, refresh the broccoli in ice water. Remove the broccoli and drain.

3. Repeat the steaming procedure with fresh water for the cauliflower. Steam for 5 to 7 minutes, until the cauliflower is tender. Remove the cauliflower from the steamer and set aside. Don't refresh it in ice water.

4. Melt the butter in a sauté pan and sauté the broccoli and cauliflower for 1 minute.

5. Combine the broccoli and cauliflower in a blender or food processor fitted with a steel blade and pulse until smooth. Add the ½ cup broth to the mixture and pulse again until smooth. You may need to add a little more broth, depending upon the consistency of the purée.

6. Serve warm or at room temperature. Freeze leftover purée that won't be eaten the next day (see page 8).

carrot purée with lemon

Their bright color and slightly sweet flavor make carrots popular with babies. The fact that they are also a major source of beta-carotene, which the body converts into vitamin A, makes them popular with parents.

Makes 2½ cups

1 pound carrots, peeled and chopped into 1-inch pieces

¼ cup whole milk

3 tablespoons unsalted butter, melted

1 teaspoon freshly squeezed lemon juice

Minced fresh parsley, for garnish (optional)

1. Bring a medium saucepan filled with water to a boil. Add the carrots and cook for 10 minutes until the carrots are tender and easily pierced with a knife. Remove the carrots with a slotted spoon and set aside.

2. In a small saucepan, combine the milk and butter and heat until the butter is melted.

3. Transfer the milk mixture to a blender with the carrots and purée until smooth. Stir in the lemon juice.

4. Garnish with the parsley and serve warm or at room temperature. Stir in 1½ cups of warmed chicken stock to transform the purée into a delicious soup for two adults. Freeze leftover purée that won't be eaten the next day (see page 8).

celery root and fresh basil purée

Celery root—or celeriac, as it is also known—is commonly prepared for babies and children in Europe. It makes good comfort food with a flavor a bit more intense than celery.

Makes 1¼ cups

1 pound celery root, peeled and cut into small cubes

2 tablespoons unsalted butter, at room temperature

10 to 15 leaves (1 ounce) fresh basil, thinly sliced, for garnish (optional)

1. Bring a large saucepan of water to a boil. Add the celery root and cook for about 10 minutes, until tender. Drain the celery root, reserving the liquid for puréeing.

2. Transfer the celery root to a blender or food processor fitted with a steel blade and purée. Add the butter and pulse until blended, adding reserved liquid if necessary to achieve the desired consistency.

3. Serve immediately. For babies one year and older sprinkle the purée with the basil. Freeze leftover purée that won't be eaten the next day (see page 8).

MY DAD

My father, André Mandion, is a pâtissier, a pastry chef well known in the southwest region of France, near Biarritz. He is a strong advocate of unprocessed food. No cooking would be his choice, the less done to the food, the better. He taught me to steam instead of boil and to use only what was fresh and in season.

—C.S.

parsnips, apples, and sweet onions

Parsnips are sweet and delicious and very popular in Europe. They are best in the fall; pick small firm ones, about five to a pound. Larger ones will need to be cored. Maui onions, which are also sweet, are a good choice for this dish. This makes a great side dish for adults.

Serves 4

1½ pounds parsnips, peeled and cut into large dice

2 tablespoons unsalted butter

1 tablespoon diced sweet onion

1½ tablespoons sugar

3 apples, such as Braeburn or Fuji, peeled, cored, and cut into bite-size pieces

1. In a medium saucepan with a steamer, bring 2 inches of water to a boil.

2. Add the parsnips to the steamer, cover, and steam for 10 minutes, until the parsnips are tender and easily pierced with a knife. Remove the parsnips from the steamer and drain.

3. In a large sauté pan over medium heat, melt the butter. Add the parsnips and onion, sprinkle them with the sugar, and cook, stirring frequently, for 5 to 8 minutes, until the parsnips are glazed and dark brown but not burned. This will reduce the bitter aftertaste of the parsnips.

4. Add the apples and cook for about 5 minutes, until tender.

5. Mash well for babies nine to twelve months old. Serve immediately.

potato and leek purée

An infant version of vichyssoise, this is for the nine-month-old—and older—baby with a discriminating palate. It can be served warm or at room temperature.

Makes 1½ cups

1 pound Yukon gold
    potatoes, peeled,
    washed, and quartered

2 leeks, trimmed, cleaned,
    and cut into 1-inch pieces

2 tablespoons unsalted
    butter

½ cup whole milk

1. In a large pot with water just to cover, boil the potatoes and leeks for about 30 minutes, until the potatoes are tender and easily pierced with the tip of a knife. Drain, reserving the water, and remove the potatoes. Pass them through a ricer. Set aside.

2. Transfer the leeks to a food processor fitted with a steel blade and purée.

3. Melt the butter in a heavy saucepan over medium heat. Add the riced potatoes. Gradually stir in the milk, beating with a wooden spoon until creamy. Stir in the puréed leeks. Stir in some of the reserved potato water for a more liquid consistency.

4. Serve immediately. Freeze leftover purée that won't be eaten the next day (see page 8).

nine to twelve months

creamed spinach

If there are any adults around when this is served, your baby will be lucky to get a nibble.

NOTES ▶ **Season with sea salt and freshly ground pepper for children over two years old and adults.**

Makes 2 cups

1 pound fresh spinach, washed and stemmed

1 shallot, minced, or 1 tablespoon minced onion

¼ cup unsalted butter

1 tablespoon all-purpose flour

1 cup heavy cream

¼ cup low-sodium chicken broth, for puréeing

1. Heat a large sauté pan over medium-high heat. Add the spinach with just the water that clings to its leaves. Add the shallot and cook, turning the spinach frequently with tongs, for about 3 minutes, until bright green. Remove the spinach and shallot from the pan and let cool. Finely chop and set aside.

2. In the same pan over medium-high heat, melt the butter and add the flour. Cook for 2 minutes, stirring constantly with a whisk. Decrease the heat to medium, add the cream, and whisk until smooth. Cook for 1 to 2 minutes. Add the spinach, stirring frequently with a wooden spoon until well blended.

3. For babies nine to twelve months, purée the mixture in a blender, adding the broth until the mixture is smooth. For older babies and adults, don't purée.

4. Serve warm. Freeze leftovers that won't be eaten the next day (see page 8).

fresh sweet peas and ham

The salty flavor of the ham makes a good contrast with the sweetness of the peas. Seek out nitrate-free ham, which is now widely available.

Serves 4

3 cups freshly shelled peas

¼ cup low-sodium chicken broth, plus extra warm broth for puréeing

4 ounces good-quality, low-sodium, nitrate-free ham, cut into ¼-inch dice

1 tablespoon unsalted butter

1. Bring a medium saucepan filled with water to a boil over high heat. Add the peas and cook for about 3 minutes, until bright green and tender. Drain and refresh in ice water. When cool, drain the peas, and set aside.

2. Heat the ¼ cup broth to a boil in small saucepan, decrease to a simmer, and add the ham. Cook for 1 minute, and then add the cooked peas, stirring for about 2 minutes, until warm. Stir in the butter.

3. Serve immediately. For babies nine to twelve months old, purée the peas and ham in a blender with the extra warmed chicken broth. Add more broth, if necessary, to achieve the desired consistency. Freeze leftovers that won't be eaten the next day (see page 8).

DEVELOPING TASTES

Although they are fraternal twins and began life eating exactly the same things, Nicolas loves Brie and Camembert, but Stephane hates it. Nicolas also loves mustard and pickles. There are always going to be differences in taste.

—C.S.

turnips, pears, and parsley

Ripe pears and a little sugar caramelize and transform the simple turnip. Make sure the pears are very ripe. For adults, this makes a great side dish for chicken, duck, or quail.

Serves 4

1½ pounds turnips, peeled and cut into cubes

2 tablespoons unsalted butter

¼ cup sugar

2 ripe Bartlett pears, peeled, cored, and quartered

Minced fresh parsley, for garnish (optional)

1. Bring a large saucepan half filled with water to a boil. Add the turnips and decrease the heat to medium-high. Cook for 10 to 12 minutes, until the turnips are tender but firm. Remove the turnips from the water and set aside to drain.

2. Melt the butter in a sauté pan over medium-high heat. Add the turnips; sprinkle them with the sugar, and cook, turning frequently, for about 5 minutes, until they are tender and caramelized. Add the pears and sauté for about 2 minutes more.

3. Mash for babies nine to eighteen months old. Garnish with parsley and serve immediately.

black beans and banana with crème fraîche

I first encountered black beans in Miami. The sweet banana and the slightly tart crème fraîche offer a nice contrast to each other and the beans. Crème fraîche, which is tangier than plain cream and less sour than sour cream, can be purchased in most grocery stores.

Serves 4

2 tablespoons extra virgin olive oil

½ medium onion, minced

1½ cups black beans, rinsed and picked over

8 cups low-sodium chicken broth

Leaves of 2 sprigs fresh thyme

2 ripe bananas, cubed

Crème fraîche, for garnish (optional)

1. Heat the oil in a large, heavy-bottomed pan over medium-high heat for 1 minute. Add the onion and sauté for about 3 minutes, until translucent.

2. Add the beans, broth, and thyme leaves, and bring to a boil. Decrease the heat to medium, cover, and cook for 1½ hours, until the beans are tender and most of the liquid has been absorbed. Check occasionally to skim any foam from the surface, if necessary.

3. To serve, place a serving of beans into a bowl and top with the banana pieces. Mash for babies younger than one year. Garnish with 1 teaspoon crème fraîche for babies older than one year and adults.

couscous with cauliflower and carrots

Despite being rich in vitamins and fiber, this is a dish our boys actually like quite a bit.

NOTES ▷ **Sea salt is included as an option for children over two years old and adults.**

Serves 4

4 carrots, peeled and finely chopped

1 cup finely chopped cauliflower florets

1⅓ cups low-sodium chicken broth

1½ tablespoons unsalted butter

1 cup couscous

Sea salt (optional)

1. In a medium saucepan with a steamer, bring 2 inches of water to a boil.

2. Add the carrots and cauliflower and steam for 10 to 12 minutes, until the vegetables are tender. Drain and set aside.

3. In a small pan, heat the broth over medium-high heat.

4. Melt the butter in a medium saucepan over medium-high heat. Stir in the couscous, stirring to coat well with the butter, and cook for 1 minute. Add the broth, cover, and cook over low heat for about 4 minutes, until the broth is absorbed. Stir in the carrots and cauliflower. Season with salt.

5. Serve slightly warm or at room temperature. Freeze leftovers than won't be eaten the next day (see page 8).

salmon with couscous and roasted green onions

This makes a quick, nutritious dinner. Use a quick-cooking couscous to have dinner prepared in about 10 minutes.

NOTES ▶ Since this is a dish the entire family will enjoy, an option for using sea salt is included in the recipe for children over two years old and adults.

Serves 4

GREEN ONIONS

1 bunch green onions, roots and ends trimmed

2 tablespoons extra virgin olive oil

Pinch of sea salt (optional)

SALMON

½ cup water

Juice of ½ lemon

¼ cup unsalted butter

4 (6-ounce) salmon steaks

COUSCOUS

4 tablespoons butter

1½ cups couscous

2¼ cups vegetable broth, warmed

½ teaspoon sea salt (optional)

1. Preheat the oven to 400°F. Rub a baking sheet with olive oil.

2. Brush the onions with the oil, place them on the baking sheet and season with salt. Roast for about 5 minutes, until bright green and tender.

3. To prepare the salmon, in a medium sauté pan, bring the water and lemon juice to a boil. Add the butter and salmon steaks. Decrease the heat to medium and cover. Poach the steaks for about 8 minutes, and then turn them carefully to cook the other side. Remove from the heat and set aside.

4. To prepare the couscous, melt 3 tablespoons of the butter in a saucepan over medium heat. Add the couscous and stir until it is coated with the butter. Pour the vegetable broth into the couscous and add the salt. Bring the mixture to a boil, then decrease the heat to a simmer. Cover and cook for 5 to 7 minutes, until all the liquid is absorbed. Remove from the heat and stir in the remaining tablespoon of butter. Cover and set aside.

5. To serve, place the couscous on a platter, arrange the salmon steaks on top, and lay the roasted green onions over the salmon steaks. Mash the salmon with the couscous for babies nine months to a year old and omit the onions.

focaccia

The fragrance of focaccia warm from the oven transports me to a little wood-paneled bakery in Italy. For adults, this is especially good employed in a sandwich with prosciutto and cheese.

NOTES	Babies nine months and older can chew on pieces of the focaccia. Sea salt is included in this recipe for children over two years old and adults.

Makes 16 (3-inch square) pieces

STARTER

1 package (2½ teaspoons) active dry yeast

½ cup warm water

1⅓ cups all-purpose flour

DOUGH

2 teaspoons active dry yeast

⅓ cup plus 1 tablespoon warm water

⅓ cup extra virgin olive oil, plus 3 tablespoons for drizzling

5 fresh sage leaves, finely chopped, plus 4 leaves finely chopped for finishing

1 teaspoon fine sea salt (optional)

2 cups all-purpose flour

1 teaspoon coarse sea salt (optional)

1. To make the starter, mix the yeast with the water in a mixing bowl and whisk. Let it stand for 10 minutes. Stir in the flour and beat until the mixture is smooth. Cover the bowl with plastic wrap and let the starter rise for about 30 minutes. It will double in size.

2. To make the dough, mix the yeast and water together, then add the ⅓ cup oil, 5 chopped sage leaves, and fine sea salt, and mix well. Stir in the starter mixture and the flour, ½ cup at a time, until the dough is soft and slightly sticky. Transfer the dough to a lightly floured surface and knead, adding more flour if necessary. The dough should be smooth and elastic.

3. Place the dough in a large, lightly oiled bowl, cover tightly with plastic wrap, and let rise for 30 minutes.

4. Punch the dough down, and roll it out to a 1 inch thick and 12 inches square, to fit in a sheet pan. (You will not cover the entire length of the sheet pan.) Cover and let rise for 1 hour.

5. Preheat the oven to 400°F. If you have one, place a baking stone in the oven according to the directions.

6. With your fingertips, make indentations all over the surface of the dough (these will collect the olive oil and salt). Spray the surface with water, drizzle with the 3 tablespoons oil, and scatter with the coarse sea salt and the 4 leaves chopped sage.

7. Place the pan in the oven, or if using a baking stone, slide the focaccia onto the baking stone. Spray the

oven with cold water three times during the first 10 minutes of baking to create steam. Bake the focaccia for about 25 minutes, until golden brown.

8. Let the focaccia rest for 10 minutes. Cut it into 3-inch squares and serve warm. Leftover focaccia can be wrapped in plastic and refrigerated for up to 2 days or frozen for up to 2 weeks. Let defrost at room temperature for about ½ hour and reheat at 350°F for about 10 minutes, until warmed through.

sweet potato risotto

Arborio rice, which is grown in the north of Italy, is the rice traditionally used to make authentic risotto. The fat, starchy grains give the dish its characteristic creamy texture. Other short-grain rice can be substituted, but the results will not be as satisfying. When preparing this for babies under two years old, substitute a less salty cheese, such as Cheddar, for the Parmesan.

Serves 4 to 6

4 large sweet potatoes

5½ cups low-sodium chicken broth

4 tablespoons unsalted butter

½ cup minced onion

1½ cups Arborio rice

½ cup grated Parmesan cheese

Leaves of 1 sprig fresh thyme

1. Preheat the oven to 375°F.

2. Wash the sweet potatoes, pierce each several times with the tip of a knife and bake for about 1 to 1½ hours, until tender. Remove them from the oven and let cool. Peel the sweet potatoes and transfer the flesh to a food processor fitted with a steel blade. Purée until smooth.

3. Heat the broth in a saucepan over low heat.

4. In a large pan, melt 1 tablespoon of the butter over medium-high heat. Add the onion and sauté for about 3 minutes, until translucent. Decrease the heat to low. Add the rice and, using a wooden spoon, stir for 2 minutes, until all the grains are well coated. Stir in the broth, ½ cup at a time. When each addition of broth is almost completely absorbed, add the next ½ cup, stirring frequently. Continue adding the broth until it has all been added and absorbed and the rice is tender but firm.

5. Stir in the puréed sweet potatoes, the cheese, the remaining 3 tablespoons of butter, and thyme leaves. Stir until creamy. Serve warm. Freeze leftovers that won't be eaten the next day (see page 8).

Nibbles

banana peach compote

Bananas are rich in potassium and fiber and one of the easiest foods to prepare for your baby. This is best, of course, with fresh, ripe peaches.

NOTES	**Purée for babies, depending on their ability to chew. For adults, serve this over granola for breakfast or with pound cake for dessert.**

Makes 3½ cups

½ cup water

6 tablespoons sugar

1 teaspoon freshly squeezed
   lemon juice

1 strip lemon zest (optional)

4 large fresh peaches, peeled,
   pitted, and quartered

2 ripe bananas, cut into
   1-inch cubes

½ cup plain yogurt

1. In a medium saucepan, combine the water and sugar and bring to a simmer, swirling the pan once or twice. When the sugar has dissolved, add the lemon juice and zest.

2. Decrease the heat until the syrup is barely simmering; add the peaches and cook, uncovered, for about 15 minutes, until the peaches are tender. Remove the pan from the heat and let the peaches cool in the liquid for 30 minutes. Remove the cooled peaches with a slotted spoon, and chop into small pieces and place in a bowl.

3. With a wooden spoon, carefully fold the banana and yogurt into the peaches until blended. Serve immediately. Freeze leftovers that won't be eaten the next day (see page 8).

3 Bites

one to two years

by the time they were a year old our boys were eating almost exactly what we were eating, with a few modifications. This is also when their particular food fetishes began to develop.

Serving sizes, other than for purées, are for two adults and two to four children, depending on the ages of the children and whether the dish will be served as a main course or side dish for adults.

green, brown, and pink lentils with apple-smoked bacon | 48

brown rice with hazelnut and apple purée | 50

grits and spinach with california cheddar | 51

chicken pot pie | 52

white fish and basil in mashed potatoes | 55

cheddar cheese muffins | 57

crème caramel | 59

banana purée with ground hazelnuts | 60

peach honey compote with lemon or lime | 61

plum honey compote | 62

rice pudding | 63

green, brown, and pink lentils with apple-smoked bacon

Many of the dishes of my childhood were flavored with bacon, and I naturally used it in the dishes I prepared for my boys after they were a year old. It's now possible to buy nitrate-free bacon, which makes using it more attractive.

Serves 4

¼ pound apple-smoked bacon, finely chopped

1 medium onion, minced

2 carrots, peeled and diced

1 celery stalk, trimmed and thinly sliced

1½ cups low-sodium chicken broth

2 cups water

½ cup brown lentils, rinsed and picked over

½ cup green lentils, rinsed and picked over

½ cup pink lentils, rinsed and picked over

Leaves from 1 sprig fresh thyme

1. In a large, heavy pot over medium heat, cook the bacon for about 4 minutes, until the fat is translucent. Add the onion and sauté for about 3 minutes, until it is soft. Stirring with a wooden spoon, add the carrots and celery and cook for 2 minutes.

2. Add the broth, water, lentils, and thyme leaves. Cover, decrease the heat to medium, and cook for about 30 minutes, until the lentils are tender and most of the liquid is absorbed.

3. Serve immediately. Freeze leftovers that won't be eaten the next day (see page 8).

brown rice with hazelnut and apple purée

This was one of our boys' favorite dishes, and it's a good way to safely introduce nuts—which are full of essential fatty acids, B vitamins, and vitamin E—into their diet.

NOTES	▶ Before you purée it for your baby, put a little in a bowl with a few hazelnut pieces and raisins for your own breakfast. If there is a family history of allergies to nuts, wait until your child is three to introduce them.

Makes 2 cups

¼ cup hazelnuts (optional)

2 cups water

1 cup brown rice

2 Braeburn or Rome apples,
   peeled, cored, and cut
   into 1-inch pieces

1 tablespoon sugar

½ cup apple juice

1. Preheat the oven to 400°F. Place the hazelnuts on a sheet pan and toast for about 10 minutes, until lightly browned. Remove and let cool.

2. In a large saucepan, bring the 2 cups water to a boil. Add the rice, cover, and reduce the heat to a simmer. Cook for about 40 minutes, until the rice is tender and the water is absorbed. Remove from the heat.

3. In a medium saucepan, combine the apples with water just to cover. Add the sugar and cook over high heat for about 8 minutes, until the apples are tender. Drain.

4. While the apples are cooking, finely grind the toasted hazelnuts in a mini blender or a food processor fitted with a steel blade.

5. Fold the apples into the cooked rice. Transfer the rice-apple mixture into a food processor fitted with a steel blade and pulse, gradually adding the apple juice, until smooth. Transfer the mixture to a bowl and fold in the hazelnuts.

6. Serve immediately. Freeze leftover purée that won't be eaten the next day (see page 8).

one to two years

grits and spinach with california cheddar

Years ago I did a consulting job in Georgia, where I was introduced to grits with gravy. Grits are very similar to polenta and the texture is great for babies. Good quality grits, which are white and coarsely ground, can be found at high-end grocery stores, health food stores, and online. Recommended Cheddars are Bravo from California, or Herkimer, from upstate New York, but any good-quality Cheddar will work well.

Serves 4

8 ounces fresh spinach, washed and stemmed

3 cups water

¾ cup good-quality grits

1 tablespoon unsalted butter

¾ cup grated good-quality Cheddar

1. In a sauté pan over medium heat, cook the spinach with just the water that clings to its leaves for 2 to 3 minutes, until the spinach is wilted and bright green. Remove the spinach and refresh in ice water. When the spinach is cool, drain it and squeeze out the excess moisture. Very finely chop it and set aside.

2. In a medium saucepan, combine the water and grits and bring to a boil over medium-high heat. Decrease the heat to a simmer and stir with a wire whisk to eliminate any lumps. Cover and cook, stirring occasionally with a wooden spoon, 5 to 10 minutes for quick-cooking grits, 15 to 20 minutes for regular grits, until all the water is absorbed.

3. Decrease the heat to a minimum and stir in the butter. Add the cheese, stirring until it is melted. Stir in the spinach.

4. Serve immediately. Freeze leftovers that won't be eaten the next day (see page 8).

chicken pot pie

This is a great one-dish lunch or dinner for the entire family. Phyllo dough can be used for convenience, or use your favorite pie crust recipe. Mash the filling with a little of the crust for babies who aren't ready for lumpy food.

Serves 6

2 pounds boneless, skinless chicken breasts or thighs

¾ cup freshly shelled peas

5½ tablespoons unsalted butter, plus 1 tablespoon melted

15 pearl onions, peeled

3 medium carrots, peeled and cut into ¼-inch pieces

2 small celery stalks, trimmed and cut into ¼-inch pieces

½ cup all-purpose flour

1½ cups whole milk

Sea salt and freshly ground black pepper (optional)

½ teaspoon fresh thyme leaves

1 (16-ounce) package phyllo dough (defrosted as per instructions on box)

1. Bring a medium saucepan of lightly salted water to a boil. Meanwhile, cut the chicken into 1-inch cubes. Add the chicken and cook, uncovered, for about 5 minutes, until tender. Drain the meat and transfer it to a large bowl. Reserve the broth and set aside.

2. Bring a medium saucepan of lightly salted water to a boil. Add the peas and cook for about 2 to 3 minutes, until the peas are bright green and tender. Drain and refresh in ice water. When cool, drain the peas and set aside.

3. Melt 1½ tablespoons of the butter in a sauté pan over medium-high heat. Add the onions, carrots, and celery, and sauté about 5 minutes. Add ¼ cup of the reserved chicken broth, and cook for 5 more minutes. Drain the vegetables and set aside.

4. Melt 4 tablespoons of the butter in a heavy-bottomed saucepan over medium heat. Stir in the flour and cook for about 3 minutes, until the mixture browns. Decrease the heat to a simmer and slowly add 2 cups of the reserved broth, whisking until smooth. Whisk in the milk and simmer, continuing to whisk until the sauce thickens. Season with salt and pepper.

5. Fold the chicken, sautéed vegetables, and peas into the sauce with a wooden spoon and mix well. Stir in the thyme. (The dish can be made to this point one day in advance. Remove the mixture from the refrigerator and let it reach room temperature before topping it with the pastry.)

6. Pour the mixture into six individual 5-inch ovenproof baking dishes or one 9 by 11 by 1¾-inch baking dish.

(continued on page 54)

one to two years

CONTINUED FROM PAGE 52

7. Preheat the oven to 400°F. Unroll six to seven sheets of phyllo dough for each dish. Cut the dough to fit the inside dimensions of the dish.

8. Fill the baking dish (or dishes) with the chicken mixture and lay one sheet of phyllo dough on top. Brush lightly with the 1 tablespoon melted butter. To prevent the edges from cracking, lightly brush the edges first and work in toward the center. Repeat for each layer, including the top layer. The pie, or pies, can be frozen at this point and baked later.

9. Bake individual pies for about 15 minutes, one large pie for 20 to 30 minutes, until the pastry is golden brown and the filling is bubbling.

10. Let cool slightly and serve. The large or individual pies can be frozen before being baked. To bake, the pie or pies should be removed from the refrigerator 1 hour before.

PROTEIN

Red meat was only on the menu about once a week, and occasionally we would serve the boys liver for the iron. Poultry showed up in dishes like Chicken Pot Pie (page 52) and Roasted Young Turkey with Pumpkin Risotto Stuffing (page 99). They ate lots of fish because it's such a good source of protein and so easy to digest. They loved White Fish and Basil with Mashed Potatoes (page 55)—it was a big favorite.   —C.S.

white fish and basil in mashed potatoes

Any white, flaky fish fresh from the market can be used for this dish. This is a simple version of brandade, a French Provençal dish served as either a main course or side dish. Prepare the mashed potatoes first so they are ready for the poached fish. Sea salt and pepper are included in the recipe for children over two years old and adults.

Serves 4

MASHED POTATOES

1 pound Yukon gold
   potatoes, peeled and
   quartered

½ cup whole milk

¼ cup unsalted butter

1¼ cups yogurt

Sea salt and freshly ground
   black pepper (optional)

WHITE FISH

Water

1½ pounds white fish fillets,
   such as ling cod or halibut

Sea salt and freshly ground
   black pepper (optional)

¼ cup extra virgin olive oil

Juice of ½ lemon

1 tablespoon thinly sliced
   fresh basil, for garnish
   (optional)

1. Bring a large pot of lightly salted water to a boil. Add the potatoes and boil for 20 to 30 minutes, until the potatoes are tender and easily pierced with a knife. Drain the potatoes and set aside to cool. When cool enough to handle, press the potatoes through a ricer.

2. Preheat the oven to 250°F.

3. In the same large pot, heat the milk and butter. Return the potatoes to the pot and stir until smooth. Add the yogurt and continue to stir. Season with salt and pepper. Cover the potatoes with aluminum foil and place in the oven to keep warm.

4. To prepare the fish, season the fillets with salt and pepper, and in a large sauté pan combine ½ inch water with the oil and lemon juice and bring to a boil. Decrease the heat to medium and cook for 1 minute. Place the fillets in the water and cover. Decrease the heat to a simmer and poach the fish for about 5 minutes, until flaky.

5. To serve, for children one to three years old flake a portion of the fish and blend it into the mashed potatoes. For adults, place a portion of mashed potatoes on individual plates and position a piece of white fish on top. Pour the reserved natural juices from the pan over the fish and for adults garnish with the basil.

cheddar cheese muffins

My boys love it when I can persuade my wife to make these. Warm, cheesy muffins are a great way to start the day, and they're rich in protein and calcium. We've found that we get the best results with Arrowhead cornmeal.

| NOTES | ▷ | The salt can be left out for children under two years old. |

**Makes 18 regular or
36 mini muffins**

10 green onions, roots and
ends trimmed

Olive oil for coating onions

1 cup whole milk

½ cup buttermilk

1 large egg

1¾ cups all-purpose flour

1 cup yellow cornmeal

¼ cup sugar

2 teaspoons baking powder

½ teaspoon baking soda

½ teaspoon sea salt
(optional)

½ cup unsalted butter

1½ cups shredded good-
quality Cheddar cheese

1. Preheat the oven to 400°F. Rub a baking sheet with oil.

2. Lightly coat the onions with olive oil, place them on the baking sheet, and season with salt. Roast for 5 to 8 minutes, until lightly browned. Chop into small dice.

3. Decrease the oven temperature to 375°F. Grease the cups of the muffin tins with butter; you can use either regular-size or mini muffin tins.

4. In a small bowl, whisk together the milk, buttermilk, and egg.

5. In a separate bowl, combine the flour, cornmeal, sugar, baking powder, baking soda, and salt.

6. In the bowl of a stand mixer fitted with the paddle attachment, cream the butter on high speed until smooth. Continuing to beat on low speed, add the flour mixture alternating with the milk mixture until smooth. Add the cheese and green onions. Mix just to blend.

7. Use a small ice-cream scoop, or measure 2 table-spoons of batter into each cup of the regular muffin tins or about 1 tablespoon of batter into the mini. Bake on the center rack of the oven for about 20 minutes for the regular size, 15 minutes for the mini, until the tops are golden and a toothpick inserted into the center comes out clean.

8. Let cool on a rack for 5 minutes before serving warm. Left over muffins can be refrigerated for up to 2 days or frozen for up to 2 weeks.

crème caramel

Who, child or adult, doesn't love crème caramel? Traditional in Europe and in Mexico, where it is known as flan, crème caramel has always been a favorite treat for our boys. To make a richer version for older children and adults, substitute cream for the milk.

Serves 6

CARAMEL

1 cup sugar

¼ cup water

1 tablespoon lemon juice

CUSTARD

3 large eggs

3 egg yolks

¾ cup sugar

4 cups whole milk, heated

1 vanilla bean

1. To make the caramel, combine the sugar, water, and lemon juice in a small, nonaluminum saucepan and bring to a simmer. Without stirring, let the sugar dissolve into a clear liquid and cover the pan.

2. Boil the syrup for several minutes over medium-high heat, again without stirring, until the bubbles are thick. Uncover the pan and continue boiling, swirling the pan occasionally.

3. As the syrup begins to color, continue to swirl the pan until the syrup is an even golden brown. Remove the pan from the heat and continue swirling. Immediately pour the caramel into a baking dish; tip to coat the bottom and halfway up the sides of the pan.

4. Preheat the oven to 350°F.

5. To make the custard, blend the eggs, yolks, and sugar in a bowl with a whisk, being careful to avoid creating foam. Gradually blend in the heated milk to dissolve the sugar completely, stirring carefully to minimize foam. Split the vanilla bean lengthwise and scrape the seeds into the bowl. Add the bean to the mixture, cover, and let steep for 10 minutes. Discard the vanilla bean and pour the mixture through a strainer into the baking dish with the caramel. Skim off any bubbles from the top.

6. Set the baking dish in a larger pan, and fill the larger pan with hot water to halfway up the side of the baking dish. Set the pan in the oven and check occasionally to make sure the water remains at a simmer.

(continued on page 60)

Bites

CONTINUED FROM PAGE 59

Boiling water will make the custard grainy. After 45 to 50 minutes, check the center with a toothpick; it should come out clean but the custard will still wiggle a bit.

7. Let the custard cool to room temperature. To serve, run a thin knife between the custard and the baking dish, invert a serving plate on top of the baking dish, and turn it over. The custard will slip out and the caramel will pool around the bottom. Cut into wedges and spoon some of the caramel over each piece. Leftovers, should there be any, can be stored in the refrigerator for up to 2 days.

banana purée with ground hazelnuts

Ground hazelnuts add nutrition and interest to simple puréed bananas.

NOTES **If there is a family history of allergies to nuts, wait until your child is three to introduce them.**

Makes 1½ cups

¼ cup hazelnuts (optional)

4 ripe bananas, puréed or mashed

1 tablespoon freshly squeezed lemon juice

1. Preheat the oven to 400°F.

2. Place the hazelnuts on a sheet pan and toast for about 10 minutes, until lightly browned. Let cool, then finely grind the nuts in a food processor fitted with a blender or a steel blade.

3. Add the bananas and pulse until well blended. Add the lemon juice and pulse a few more times to blend.

4. Serve immediately. Freeze leftovers that won't be eaten the next day (see page 8).

one to two years

peach honey compote with lemon or lime

Make this only when you have fresh peaches at the peak of the season.

NOTES ▶ **Remember, no honey for babies under a year.**

Serves 4

¼ cup water

2 tablespoons good-quality honey

1 teaspoon freshly squeezed lemon or lime juice

4 large or 6 medium ripe peaches, peeled, pitted, and finely chopped

1. In a medium saucepan, combine the water, honey, and lemon juice. Bring to a boil and boil for 1 minute.

2. Decrease the heat to a simmer and add the peaches. Cook for about 5 minutes, depending on the ripeness of the fruit, until the peaches are tender but not mushy. Let cool.

3. Serve at room temperature. Leftovers can be refrigerated for up to 2 days or frozen for up to 2 months (see page 8).

FEEDING WHILE TRAVELING

At four months old, our boys went with us to Europe for my sister's wedding. For the plane trip I brought prepared organic baby food, which worked well. We have traveled abroad with the boys every summer. In Europe, we take the kids to restaurants and they eat a little of what we are having; there are no children's menus in Europe.   —C.S.

---

plum honey compote

Any stone fruit in season can be used in this compote: cherries, peaches, or apricots.

> **NOTES** ▶ **Because this contains honey, it's not suitable for children younger than a year old.**

Serves 4

1 cup water

1 teaspoon freshly squeezed
   lemon juice

½ cup honey

16 assorted plums, peeled,
   pitted, and cut into
   ½-inch pieces

¼ cup golden raisins

Zest of 1 lemon

1 strip orange zest

1. In a large saucepan, combine the water, lemon juice, and honey and bring to a boil. Boil for 3 minutes.

2. Add the plums, raisins, lemon zest, and orange zest. Decrease the heat to a simmer. Cook for about 5 minutes, until the plums are tender but not mushy. Watch the plums closely; depending on their freshness, they can become too soft very quickly. Let cool.

3. Serve at room temperature. Leftovers can be refrigerated for up to 2 days or frozen for up to 2 months (see page 8).

DINING OUT WITH THE KIDS

The main thing about dining in restaurants with your babies is not to mind that no one is enjoying the antics of your adorable children quite as much as you are (and that's probably not very much). The brief window of time when they're young enough to sleep through a meal in their carrier closes at about four months. Being the offspring of restaurateurs and very busy people, our boys, Nicolas and Stephane, probably have spent more time in restaurants than most of their peers. They were taught the social aspects of civilized dining early in their lives. We would usually end up in Monterey Park, a neighborhood near ours, which is famous for its very good and very large Chinese restaurants. In a very large restaurant, you're not as likely to be the center of attention. Chinese fare is also healthy: steamed vegetables, fresh fish, and rice, some of which would usually end up all over the table. By two

rice pudding

Everyone's favorite, this pudding can be puréed if your baby is not able to manage lumps yet. Adults and older children will happily consume this with a little fruit compote—or without—for breakfast.

Serves 4

5 cups whole milk

¾ cup sugar

4 cinnamon sticks

1 cup short-grain rice

½ teaspoon ground
  cinnamon

Pinch of ground nutmeg

1. In a heavy medium saucepan, combine the milk and sugar with the cinnamon sticks and bring to a boil, stirring constantly with a whisk for about 2 minutes, until the sugar is dissolved.

2. Decrease the heat to a simmer, add the rice, cover, and cook, stirring occasionally with a wooden spoon for about 1 hour, until most of the milk has been absorbed and the texture is creamy.

3. Remove the cinnamon sticks and stir in the ground cinnamon and nutmeg.

4. Serve the pudding warm or refrigerate and serve chilled.

DINING OUT WITH THE KIDS, *continued*

and a half, however, the boys were sitting at the table and eating with utensils and not running around and pulling on tablecloths—most of the time, that is. We would usually dine late on Sunday afternoons, before the boys were cranky and the dinner crowd arrived.

Dining at ethnic restaurants, especially Chinese and Korean restaurants, exposed the boys to exotic flavors and developed their love of fresh fish. Even before they were three, they were game for anything and even tried sea cucumber, a challenge for the most sophisticated diner.   —C.S.

4 Meals

two to three years

lthough the recipes in this chapter don't constitute meals in themselves, we chose the title "Meals" because at this age our babies had grown into toddlers and were able to sit at the tables in high chairs and take part, very enthusiastically, in family meals. Serving sizes, other than for purées, are for two adults and two to four children, depending on the ages of the children and whether the dish will be served as a main course or side dish for adults.

artichokes with extra virgin
olive oil | 66

avocado with onion and
cilantro | 67

roasted beet and orange juice
purée | 68

brussels sprouts, sweet onion, and
nutmeg | 70

napa or savoy cabbage with
lemon | 71

fresh peas, onions, and
apple-smoked bacon | 73

garbanzo bean casserole | 74

white beans and parsley | 75

wild rice risotto with carrots and
celery | 76

tomato and basil risotto | 77

wild rice with mushrooms and
onions | 78

shrimp and scallop risotto | 79

grilled lobster, corn, and
red pepper | 80

tuna with baby spinach and
tomatoes | 83

classic beef stew | 84

lamb stew with carrots and
prunes | 85

braised pork with apricots and
onions | 86

biscuits | 88

bran muffins with currants, dried
cranberries, and pecans | 89

chocolate chip shortbread | 90

orange sable cookies | 91

apple apricot compote | 93

artichokes with extra virgin olive oil

Artichokes are not typical baby fare, but we always sought to broaden our babies' palates, and they were fascinated by the artichoke as an object. Leftover artichoke hearts can be used in a salad.

Serves 4

4 large artichokes

2 tablespoons freshly squeezed lemon juice

3 tablespoons extra virgin olive oil

Sea salt and freshly ground black pepper

1. Peel off the tough outer leaves of the artichoke. Trim around the base of the artichoke and cut the top leaves close to the artichoke heart without removing any flesh. Remove the fuzzy center with your fingers and, with a spoon, lightly scrape the cavity of the heart. Rub the heart with lemon juice to prevent it from discoloring.

2. In a medium saucepan with a steamer, bring 2 inches of water to a boil. Add the artichoke hearts to the steamer, cover, and cook for 15 to 25 minutes, until tender and easily pierced with the tip of a knife. Remove the cooked artichoke hearts and let cool.

3. Cut the cooled artichoke hearts into bite-size pieces and toss with the oil. Season with salt and pepper and serve.

two to three years

avocado with onion and cilantro

Living in Southern California inspired my interest in avocados; they're such an integral part of the cuisine. In addition to their wonderful taste and texture, they provide vitamins A and C and unsaturated fatty acids, which are important, I've been told, for brain development. This also makes a great dip for the rest of the family.

Makes 2 cups

2 large avocados, halved,
    peeled, and pitted

¼ tablespoon minced onion

2 tablespoons freshly
    squeezed lemon juice

Sea salt

Minced cilantro leaves for
    garnish (optional)

1. Mash the avocado with a fork in a mixing bowl until smooth. (Reserve one of the avocado pits to place in the mixture to keep the avocado from turning brown if you're not serving it right away.)

2. Mix in the minced onion, lemon juice, and sea salt.

3. To serve, remove the pit (if necessary) and garnish with the minced cilantro leaves.

PICKY EATERS

Kids can be picky eaters, and it's a great temptation to give them pasta when the meal you've prepared is rejected and you can't think of anything else. Pasta is actually very low in nutrients, so we only gave our boys pasta about once every two weeks, unless there was a little in the soup. The same goes for potatoes. As much as possible, we tried to stick with the original meal selection. If we had rushed to provide something else, we would have been sending the kids a message that says we'll keep trying until we find something acceptable. Remember the old adage: "Start out as you mean to go on." Few of us want to be juggling different foods, desperately trying to find something the kids will agree to eat, for the next eighteen years. —C.S.

roasted beet and orange juice purée

Fortunately, our boys always liked beets, maybe for the color and slightly sweet flavor. This is a good source of iron and vitamin C for babies nine months and older.

Makes 2 cups

4 medium beets, red, yellow, or orange

1 tablespoon extra virgin olive oil

¼ cup freshly squeezed orange juice

1 teaspoon orange zest strips (optional)

1. Preheat the oven to 350°F.

2. Wash the beets but do not dry them, and coat with the oil. Wrap them individually in aluminum foil and place on a baking sheet.

3. Roast the beets for 30 to 40 minutes, until tender and easily pierced with the tip of a knife. Set aside until cool enough to handle.

4. Remove the beets from the foil, peel, and cut into quarters. Place the beets into a food processor fitted with a steel blade and purée them with the orange juice.

5. Serve immediately, sprinkled with a couple strips of orange zest.

brussels sprouts, sweet onion, and nutmeg

It was always a challenge to get our kids to eat Brussels sprouts, but they are so nutritious that we've tried a number of ways to make them appealing. This was pretty successful.

NOTES ▶ **For babies twelve to eighteen months, this can be mashed or puréed in a blender or food processor with enough water to reach the desired consistency.**

Serves 4

1½ pounds Brussels sprouts, trimmed and quartered

1 tablespoon extra virgin olive oil

1 tablespoon minced sweet onion

1½ cups low-sodium chicken broth

½ teaspoon nutmeg (optional)

Sea salt and freshly ground black pepper

1. Bring a large pot of lightly salted water to a boil. Add the Brussels sprouts and cook for 10 to 12 minutes, until bright green. Drain the Brussels sprouts and refresh in ice water. When cool, remove them and set aside to drain.

2. Heat the oil in a large sauté pan over medium-high heat for 1 minute. Add the onion and Brussels sprouts and sauté for about 5 minutes, until the onion softens. Add the broth and nutmeg. Season with salt and pepper. Stir 3 to 4 minutes to heat.

3. Serve immediately.

napa or savoy cabbage with lemon

We often served our boys cabbage because it is so rich in vitamin C.

NOTES ▶	**Babies must be at least eighteen months old to eat cabbage since it can be difficult to digest.**

Serves 4

1½ pounds savoy or napa
   cabbage, cored and cut
   into ½-inch slices on the
   diagonal

1 tablespoon extra virgin
   olive oil

1 cup low-sodium chicken
   broth

1 teaspoon freshly squeezed
   lemon juice

Sea salt and freshly ground
   black pepper (optional)

1. Bring a large pot of lightly salted water to a boil and add the cabbage. Cook for 10 to 12 minutes, until the cabbage is bright green and tender. Drain the cabbage and refresh in ice water. When cool, drain and set the cabbage aside.

2. Heat the oil in a large sauté pan over moderate heat. Add the cabbage and broth. Cook for 5 to 8 minutes, until the cabbage is tender. Stir in the lemon juice and season with salt and pepper.

3. Serve immediately.

Meals

fresh peas, onions, and apple-smoked bacon

The distinctive smoked flavor of the bacon and the sweetness of the onion make this simple pea dish enticing enough for adults. Any onion can be substituted for the Maui, but sweet ones work best.

NOTES ▶ **For babies six to twelve months old, omit the onion and bacon, and purée about ½ cup of the peas in the blender with enough of the broth to achieve a smooth consistency.**

Serves 4

4 cups freshly shelled peas

⅓ pound apple-smoked bacon, finely diced

1 cup low-sodium chicken broth

1 medium Maui onion, diced

Sea salt and freshly ground black pepper

1. Bring a large saucepan of lightly salted water to a boil. Add the peas and cook for about 3 minutes, until the peas are bright green and tender, about 3 minutes. Drain the peas and refresh in ice water. When cool, drain them and set aside.

2. Refill the saucepan with water (do not add salt) and bring to a boil. Blanch the diced bacon in the water for 1 minute. Remove it from the heat, drain, and set the bacon aside.

3. Bring the broth to a boil in a large saucepan. Decrease the heat to medium-high, add the onion and bacon, and cook for 3 minutes. Stir in the peas and cook for 2 to 3 minutes, until the peas are hot.

4. Season with salt and pepper and serve immediately.

garbanzo bean casserole

This dish is a product of the time I spent in Provence, where garbanzo beans are a common ingredient in salads and stews and the wonderful cracker known as socca.

NOTES > For babies one to two years old, purée the beans in a food processor fitted with a steel blade, adding enough water to achieve the desired consistency.

Serves 4

2 cups dried garbanzo beans, rinsed and picked over

¼ cup plus 3 tablespoons extra virgin olive oil

1 tablespoon minced onion

1 tablespoon freshly squeezed lemon juice

Leaves of 1 sprig fresh thyme

Sea salt and freshly ground black pepper (optional)

1. Soak the beans in a bowl filled with cold water overnight. Rinse and drain.

2. In a large casserole, heat the ¼ cup oil over medium heat. Add the onion and cook for 3 to 4 minutes, until tender. Add the beans, lemon juice, and thyme leaves. Season with salt and pepper. Add water to cover the beans by 2 inches. Bring to a boil, then decrease the heat to medium. Cover and cook, stirring occasionally, for about two hours, depending on the age of the beans, until most of the liquid is absorbed and the beans are tender.

3. When the beans are done, stir in the 3 tablespoons oil. Adjust the seasoning if necessary. Serve immediately.

two to three years

white beans and parsley

Known as haricot blanc in France, white beans are a staple of traditional dishes like cassoulet. When cooking beans, keep in mind that cooking time is greatly affected by the age of the beans; younger beans can cook twice as fast as older ones.

> **NOTES** **For babies from one to two years old, purée the beans in a food processor fitted with a steel blade, adding more chicken stock to achieve the desired consistency.**

Serves 4

2 cups white or pinto beans, rinsed and picked over

3 tablespoons extra virgin olive oil

1 tablespoon chopped onion

6 cloves garlic, minced

½ cup finely diced apple-smoked bacon

4 to 5 cups low-sodium chicken broth

3 tablespoons finely chopped parsley

Sea salt and freshly ground black pepper

1. Soak the beans in a bowl filled with cold water overnight. Rinse and drain.

2. In a large casserole, heat the oil over medium-high heat for 1 minute. Decrease the heat to medium; add the onion, garlic, and bacon, and sauté for 2 to 3 minutes, until the bacon fat is translucent.

3. Add the broth and beans and bring to a boil. Decrease the heat and simmer for 30 to 40 minutes, until the beans are tender.

4. Stir in the parsley and season with salt and pepper. Serve immediately.

wild rice risotto with carrots and celery

Although a true risotto is made with Arborio rice, I call this a risotto because the cooking method is the same. Wild rice, which is actually a grass, adds texture and a nutty flavor, which I like.

> **NOTES** For babies seven to nine months old, purée the rice with enough chicken broth to reach the desired consistency.

Serves 4

3 tablespoons unsalted butter

1 carrot, peeled and cut into small pieces

1 celery stalk, trimmed and cut into small pieces

1½ cups wild rice, rinsed

4 cups low-sodium chicken broth, warmed

Sea salt and freshly ground black pepper

1. In a medium saucepan, melt 1 tablespoon of the butter over medium-high heat. Add the carrot and celery and sauté for 5 minutes. Decrease the heat to medium, add the rice, and cook for 1 minute, stirring constantly.

2. Add 1 cup of the broth and cook, stirring occasionally, until most of the liquid has been absorbed. At that point add another ½ cup of the broth and repeat the process for 25 to 35 minutes, until all the liquid has been absorbed. Stir in the remaining 2 tablespoons of butter.

3. Season with salt and pepper. Serve immediately.

tomato and basil risotto

Italian children are raised on risotto. You can whip up a batch with just about anything in the refrigerator. We began serving risotto to our boys when they were two years old.

Serves 4 to 6

1½ pounds Roma tomatoes

2 tablespoons extra virgin olive oil

1 tablespoon finely chopped sweet onion

2 cups Arborio rice

6 cups low-sodium chicken broth, warmed

½ cup freshly grated Parmesan cheese

2 tablespoons unsalted butter

Sea salt and freshly ground black pepper

1 tablespoon thinly sliced basil leaves, for garnish (optional)

1. Bring a large saucepan of water to a boil. Add the tomatoes and blanch for 1 minute, until the skins begin to split. Remove the tomatoes from the water and set aside to cool, then peel, seed, and chop into small pieces.

2. Heat the oil in a medium heavy-bottomed pot over medium heat for 1 minute. Add the onion and sauté for 3 to 4 minutes, until translucent and tender. Add the rice and stir to coat with the oil for 1 to 2 minutes. Reduce the heat to low.

3. Add the broth, ½ cup at a time, stirring frequently until it is absorbed by the rice. Repeat the process for 20 to 30 minutes, until the rice is tender and all the broth has been added and absorbed.

4. Stir in the tomatoes and the Parmesan until they are completely incorporated. Stir in the butter to make the mixture creamy.

5. Season with salt and pepper. Garnish with the basil for adult servings. Serve immediately.

DINING EN FAMILLE

Europeans are very traditional about mealtimes. Everyone sits down to eat together, whoever is there—the nanny, the au pair, a friend. The ritual is always the same, even though the participants may change. And there is no TV in the kitchen or dining room.   —C.S.

---

wild rice with mushrooms and onions

This is another variation on a risotto-style wild rice dish, this time with the pungent flavor of mushrooms and onions.

NOTES ▸ **For babies nine to twelve months old, purée the rice mixture with enough chicken broth to reach the desired consistency.**

Serves 4 to 6

4 cups low-sodium chicken broth

2 tablespoons extra virgin olive oil

¼ cup minced sweet onion

1 cup ¼-inch diced carrot

4 ounces shiitake, oyster, or button mushrooms, cleaned and cut into ¼-inch pieces

1½ cups wild rice, rinsed

½ cup grated Parmesan cheese

Leaves of 1 sprig fresh thyme

2 tablespoons unsalted butter, at room temperature

Sea salt and freshly ground black pepper

1. Heat the broth in a medium saucepan to a simmer over low heat.

2. In a large pot, heat the oil for 1 minute over medium-high heat. Add the onion, carrot, and mushrooms and cook for 6 to 8 minutes, until tender. Add the wild rice and stir for 1 minute to coat with the oil.

3. Pour ½ cup of the heated broth into the rice, stirring constantly. As the rice absorbs the broth, add additional broth in ½-cup increments. Repeat this process for 18 to 20 minutes until the grains are tender and puffed. Remove the pan from the heat.

4. Add the Parmesan, thyme, and butter, stirring until creamy. Season with salt and pepper and serve immediately.

shrimp and scallop risotto

Christine and I used to take the boys to Chinese restaurants with very good seafood near our neighborhood when they were as young as two. Consequently, they developed a taste for shellfish very early, especially when it's added to risotto.

Serves 4

6 cups low-sodium chicken
   or vegetable broth

6 tablespoons unsalted
   butter

½ onion, finely chopped

1½ cups Arborio rice

6 ounces medium shrimp,
   shelled and deveined

6 ounces large scallops, cut
   into quarters

1 teaspoon freshly squeezed
   lemon juice

½ cup half-and-half

Sea salt and freshly ground
   black pepper

1 tablespoon finely chopped
   parsley, for garnish
   (optional)

1. Heat the broth in a saucepan over low heat.

2. Melt 4 tablespoons of the butter in a large, heavy-bottomed pan over medium-high heat. Add the onion and sauté until tender and translucent, about 1 minute. Decrease the heat to low. Add the rice and stir with a wooden spoon until completely coated.

3. Add the broth, ½ cup at a time, stirring frequently until it is absorbed by the rice. Repeat the process for 20 to 30 minutes, until the rice is tender and all the liquid has been added and absorbed.

4. In a large sauté pan, melt the remaining 2 tablespoons of butter over medium-high heat. Add the shrimp, scallops, and lemon juice and cook for about 2 minutes, until the scallops are firm and the shrimp is pink.

5. Stirring over low heat, add the half-and-half to the risotto. Stir in the shrimp and scallops. Season with salt and pepper and garnish with parsley. Serve immediately. For children two to three years old, mince the shrimp and scallops with some rice.

grilled lobster, corn, and red pepper

Our kids' first experience with lobster was in a restaurant when they were two. We cut it up for them and mixed it with rice. They liked it so much that I developed this recipe to encourage them. The cilantro butter can be used for any grilled fish.

NOTES > If there is a family history of allergies to shellfish, wait until your child is at least three years old to introduce it. Cut lobster into tiny pieces to prevent choking. Only offer tiny bites to babies older than two years. The texture of lobster may not be appealing, and if not prepared correctly, it can be difficult to chew. Mash corn for children younger than three years. The kernels can present a choking hazard.

Serves 4

CILANTRO BUTTER

1 cup unsalted butter, softened

1 cup fresh cilantro, chopped

1 fresh red chile, seeded and chopped

1 tablespoon freshly squeezed lime juice

2 teaspoons sea salt

1 teaspoon freshly ground black pepper

PEPPERS

3 red bell peppers

VINAIGRETTE

2 tablespoons freshly squeezed lemon juice

1 teaspoon minced lemon zest

¼ teaspoon sea salt

6 tablespoons extra virgin olive oil

Freshly ground black pepper

LOBSTER

4 (1¼ pound) lobsters

½ lemon

CORN

4 ears fresh corn, shucked

1. Prepare a hot fire in a charcoal or gas grill.

2. To prepare the cilantro butter, beat the butter until creamy in the bowl of a stand mixer fitted with the paddle attachment. Add the cilantro, chile, lime juice, salt, and pepper and blend well. Transfer to a heat-proof bowl and place near the grill for brushing on the lobster.

(continued on page 82)

CONTINUED FROM PAGE **80**

3. Grill the peppers whole over flaming coals or holding with a long-handled fork over high flames on the stove, turning frequently, until the skin is charred. Place them in a bowl tightly covered with plastic wrap. Set aside for 5 to 10 minutes, until they are cool enough to handle.

4. While the peppers are cooling, prepare the vinaigrette. In a small bowl, mix together the lemon juice, zest, and sea salt. Whisk in the oil until emulsified. Season with pepper and set aside.

5. Peel the charred skin off the peppers, discard the stems and seeds, and slice the flesh into ½-inch strips. Toss the strips with the vinaigrette.

6. To cook the lobsters, bring a large stockpot of lightly salted water to a boil. Place the lobsters in the pot with the lemon and cook for 10 minutes. Remove the lobsters from the water and set aside.

7. Meanwhile, bring a couple of inches of water to a boil in a large pot. Add the corn and cook just until hot, about 5 minutes. Remove and let cool. Cut the kernels off the cob with a sharp knife and mix with the bell peppers.

8. When the lobsters are cool enough to handle, cut them in half lengthwise from the shell side and remove the head sac.

9. Grill the lobsters shell side down over medium-hot coals, frequently brushing the flesh with cilantro butter for 5 to 6 minutes, until warmed through.

10. To serve, place each lobster, flesh side up, on an individual serving plate with about a cup of peppers and corn spooned alongside.

tuna with baby spinach and tomatoes

Purchase tuna from a local fish market and look for cuts that are vibrant red. Our son Nicolas loves tuna, especially toro, the cut from the belly. He'll try any sort of seafood. His twin, Stephane, is more cautious and rarely ventures beyond salmon and other familiar fish.

> **NOTES** **For babies one to two years old, mash small pieces of tuna with the spinach.**

Serves 4 to 6

8 medium vine-ripened
  tomatoes, halved
  lengthwise

Sea salt and freshly ground
  black pepper

2 tablespoons thinly sliced
  basil leaves

½ teaspoon lemon zest strips

2 tablespoons extra virgin
  olive oil

4 (5-ounce) tuna steaks

1 pound baby spinach,
  washed and stemmed

1. Preheat the oven to 375°F. Rub a baking sheet with olive oil.

2. Place the tomato halves cut side down on the baking sheet. Season them with salt and pepper and roast for 15 minutes.

3. When cool enough to handle, slice the tomatoes and toss with the basil and lemon zest.

4. Heat 1 tablespoon of the oil in a large sauté pan over high heat. Add the tuna steaks and sear for 2 to 4 minutes on each side for rare, 8 to 10 minutes for well-done.

5. Warm a sauté pan over medium heat, add the remaining 1 tablespoon of oil, and sauté the spinach for 2 to 3 minutes, until wilted.

6. To serve, mix the spinach with the tomato and place on individual plates with the seared tuna on top.

classic beef stew

Ask the butcher for stew meat, already cut into cubes. The stew can be made a day or two ahead and kept in the refrigerator, its flavors improving as it sits. Freshly cooked pasta, such as linguine with butter, makes a good side dish.

NOTES	▶	**For babies eighteen months to three years old, cut the meat into tiny pieces and mash the vegetables.**

Serves 4 to 6

5 Roma tomatoes

1 tablespoon all-purpose
   flour

2 pounds chuck or shoulder
   beef, cut into 1-inch cubes

¼ cup extra virgin olive oil

1 clove garlic, roughly
   chopped

2 small onions, each cut into
   8 pieces

2 cups beef broth

4 cups water

Leaves of 1 sprig fresh thyme

1 bay leaf

4 medium Yukon gold
   potatoes, peeled and cut
   into 1-inch cubes

5 carrots, peeled and cut into
   1-inch pieces

Sea salt and freshly ground
   black pepper

1. Preheat the oven to 350°F.

2. Bring a medium saucepan of lightly salted water to a boil. Add the tomatoes and blanch for 1 minute, until the skins begin to split. Remove from the water and set aside to cool, then peel and quarter.

3. Sprinkle the flour on a plate and dredge the cubes of meat in it. Heat the oil in a large ovenproof casserole over medium-high heat for 1 minute. Add the garlic and cook for 1 minute. Add as many pieces of the beef to the pan as will fit in one layer without crowding; otherwise the meat will steam. Turn the meat frequently for 3 to 5 minutes, until brown on all sides. Transfer the browned pieces to a platter and continue with the remaining meat. When finished, return all the meat to the casserole.

4. Add the onions and tomatoes, stirring with a wooden spoon, and cook for 1 to 2 minutes. Pour in the beef broth and water, add the thyme and bay leaf, and bring to a boil. Cover and bake for 20 to 30 minutes.

5. Remove the casserole from the oven and add the potatoes and carrots; return to the oven and bake for about 30 minutes, until the vegetables are tender.

6. Remove the casserole from the oven and season with salt and pepper. Serve immediately.

two to three years

lamb stew with carrots and prunes

This is another good dish for making a day ahead; the flavors mingle and you can skim off even more of the fat. The carrots and prunes add a touch of sweetness, making it more palatable for kids.

| NOTES | For babies one to two years old, mince the lamb with mashed prunes and carrots. Older children can also have a little onion mixed in. |

Serves 4 to 6

¼ cup extra virgin olive oil

2 pounds boneless lamb shoulder, excess fat removed and meat cut into large cubes

2 medium sweet onions, each cut into 8 pieces

4 large carrots, peeled and cut into 1-inch pieces

2 cups vegetable broth

Leaves from 1 sprig fresh thyme

1 cup dried pitted prune halves

Sea salt and freshly ground black pepper

1. Heat the oil in a Dutch oven over high heat. Add as many pieces of the lamb as will fit in one layer without crowding; otherwise the meat will steam. Turn the meat frequently for 3 to 5 minutes until brown on all sides. Transfer the browned pieces to a platter and continue with the remaining meat.

2. Preheat the oven to 350°F.

3. Decrease the heat under the Dutch oven; add the onions and carrots, and sauté for 10 minutes, until the vegetables are soft. Pour in the broth, scraping up any browned bits that may have stuck to the bottom of the pan, and cook for 2 minutes.

4. Return the meat to the pot, add the thyme, cover, and place in the oven. Bake for 1 to 1½ hours, until the meat is almost tender. Remove the pot from the oven, add the prunes, cover, and return to the oven. Bake for about 10 minutes more, until the meat is tender.

5. Season with salt and pepper. Serve immediately.

braised pork with apricots and onions

This is best in apricot season with fresh apricots; otherwise, dried apricots—preferably organic since they don't contain chemicals—will work.

Serves 6

3 tablespoons extra virgin olive oil

2½ pounds boneless pork shoulder or butt roast

Sea salt and freshly ground black pepper

36 pearl onions, peeled

6 carrots peeled and sliced into ½-inch pieces

1 bay leaf

1 tablespoon red wine vinegar

2 cups low-sodium chicken broth, plus more if necessary

12 fresh apricots, halved and pitted

1. Preheat the oven 375°F.

2. Heat a Dutch oven over medium-high heat for 3 minutes. Add the oil. When it begins smoking, add the pork and sear for 2 to 4 minutes, until brown on all sides, seasoning with salt and pepper as it is turned.

3. Remove the pork, pour off most of the rendered fat, and decrease the heat to medium-low. Add the onions and carrots and cook for 2 to 4 minutes, until the onions are translucent and the carrots are soft. Add the bay leaf, vinegar, and 1 cup of the broth. Bring to a boil and boil for 1 minute.

4. Decrease the heat to low and return the meat to the pot. Pour in the remaining 1 cup of broth and bring to a boil. Remove from the heat, cover, and place in the oven for 45 minutes.

5. Return to the stove top and cook over low heat for about 45 minutes more, checking occasionally to make sure the vegetables don't dry out. Add a little more broth, if necessary.

6. When the meat and vegetables are tender, add the apricots and cook for 3 minutes over low heat.

7. Transfer the pork to a large bowl. Drain the vegetables and apricots, reserving the liquid, and place them in the bowl with the pork.

8. In a medium saucepan, cook the reserved liquid over high heat until reduced by half. Season with salt and pepper and return to the Dutch oven along with the meat and vegetables. Bring to a quick boil to reheat.

9. To serve, slice the pork and place each slice on an individual serving plate with some vegetables and apricots, and drizzle with the sauce.

biscuits

Biscuits are quick and versatile. They're great for breakfast with butter and jam, for dinner as an accompaniment to Chicken Pot Pie, or as dessert, smothered in fresh sliced strawberries with a dollop of whipped cream.

Makes about 12 biscuits

2 cups all-purpose flour

1 tablespoon baking soda

1 teaspoon sea salt

⅓ cup unsalted butter, plus additional melted butter for brushing tops

1 cup buttermilk

1. Preheat the oven to 350°F. Lightly grease a baking sheet with butter.

2. Combine the flour, baking soda, and salt in the bowl of a stand mixer fitted with the paddle attachment and mix on low speed. Add the ⅓ cup butter and mix until a very coarse meal forms. Add the buttermilk and continue to mix on low speed just to combine. Be careful not to overmix.

3. Turn the dough out onto a lightly floured work surface and pat out to about a ¾-inch-think rectangle. Using a metal biscuit cutter or a glass, cut out 2-inch rounds. Press together the remaining dough and repeat the process to use it up. Place the biscuits about an inch apart on the baking sheet and brush the tops with melted butter.

4. Bake for 12 minutes, or until the tops are golden.

5. Let the biscuits cool briefly on a wire rack before serving.

DESSERT

Dessert is not an established part of our meals. It's typically French to end a meal with something sweet, and it's a habit I had to break. It's not good for the digestion, and it develops an unhealthy expectation. On rare occasions, the boys were allowed ice cream or a cookie. The scarcity of dessert made it useful for bribery if lunch or dinner was not going well. It still is.   —C.S.

two to three years

bran muffins with currants, dried cranberries, and pecans

Muffins are a healthy alternative to cupcakes and cookies. Also, they can be baked ahead and frozen, which is perfect for a busy morning.

Makes 18 regular or 36 mini muffins

½ cup pecans, finely chopped

2⅓ cups all-purpose flour

1 cup wheat bran

1 cup firmly packed light brown sugar

2½ teaspoons baking soda

½ teaspoon baking powder

½ teaspoon sea salt

2 large eggs

½ cup canola oil

1½ cups buttermilk

½ cup currants, finely chopped

½ cup cranberries, finely chopped

1. Preheat the oven to 425°F.

2. Arrange the pecans on a sheet pan in a single layer and toast for 6 to 8 minutes, turning over once, until browned and fragrant. When cool, chop finely.

3. Decrease the oven temperature to 375°F. Grease the cups of the muffin tins with canola oil; you can use either regular-size or mini muffin tins.

4. In a medium bowl, combine the flour, bran, sugar, baking soda, baking powder, and salt.

5. In a separate bowl, mix the eggs, oil, and buttermilk. Add the flour mixture and blend. Fold in the currants, cranberries, and pecans.

6. Use a small ice cream scoop or measure two tablespoons of batter into each of the regular muffin tins or about 1 tablespoon of batter into the mini. Bake on the center rack of the oven for about 20 minutes for the regular size or 15 minutes for the mini, until the tops are golden and a toothpick inserted in the center of one of the muffins comes out clean.

7. Let cool on a rack for about 5 minutes before serving warm. Put extras in a freezer bag (no plastic wrap), date them, freeze, and use them within a month.

chocolate chip shortbread

This is Christine's recipe. She's the daughter of an acclaimed French pâtissier, (pastry chef), so it must be in her genes. Or maybe she just inherited the recipe.

 NOTES > Cookies with chocolate chips are suitable for children over two. Chocolate can be difficult to digest.

Makes about 2½ dozen

1 cup unsalted butter, cut
    into pieces

½ cup sugar

2 cups all-purpose flour

Pinch of sea salt

4 ounces semisweet
    chocolate chips

1. In the bowl of a stand mixer fitted with the paddle attachment, beat the butter and sugar on high speed for about 5 minutes, until light and fluffy.

2. Sift the flour and salt together into a bowl. Add to the butter-sugar mixture and beat on low speed, pausing to scrape down the sides of the bowl, and continuing to beat on low speed until the dough is smooth. Add the chocolate chips and beat just to blend.

3. Roll the dough into two logs 1½ inches thick and about 11 inches long. Wrap them tightly in plastic wrap and chill for 1 hour. (They may also be frozen for up to 2 weeks. If frozen, defrost in the refrigerator overnight to use.)

4. Preheat the oven to 250°F. Line a baking sheet with parchment paper.

5. Cut the logs into ⅜-inch-thick slices and place 1 inch apart on the baking sheet.

6. Bake for about 40 minutes, until firm and lightly golden brown around the edges. Transfer to a rack to cool.

two to three years

orange sable cookies

The orange zest adds a refreshing flavor to these cookies. We didn't start giving our boys cookies until they were about two, and then very seldom.

Makes about 5 dozen

4 cups all-purpose flour

1½ cups confectioners' sugar

Pinch of fine sea salt

¾ cup unsalted butter

Zest of 2 oranges, finely minced

1 cup raw sugar, to coat

1. Sift together the flour, confectioners' sugar, and salt.

2. In the bowl of a stand mixer fitted with the paddle attachment, cream the butter on high speed for about 3 minutes, until light and fluffy. Add the orange zest and beat on low speed for 1 minute. With the mixer on low speed, add the flour mixture, pausing to scrape down the sides of the bowl. Continue to beat just until the dough is smooth. Be careful not to overbeat.

3. Divide the dough into three equal portions. Roll each into a log about 1½ inches thick and 5 inches long. Pour the raw sugar onto a sheet pan and roll the logs in it to coat evenly. Wrap each log in plastic wrap. Refrigerate for 1 hour. (The logs may be frozen for up to 2 weeks. If frozen, defrost in the refrigerator overnight to use.)

4. Preheat the oven to 375°F. Line a baking sheet with parchment paper.

5. Cut the dough into ⅜-inch-thick slices and place on the baking sheet.

6. Bake for 8 to 10 minutes, until the edges turn light golden brown. Transfer to a rack to cool.

apple apricot compote

Fresh apricots are really necessary for the success of this compote. Dried apricots make the texture too chewy.

Serves 4

1 cup water

1 teaspoon freshly squeezed
   lemon juice

¼ cup sugar

2 Braeburn, Cortland, or
   Jonagold apples, peeled,
   cored, and cut into
   ½-inch pieces

8 fresh apricots, pitted and
   cut into ½-inch pieces

1 strip lemon zest (optional)

1. In a medium saucepan, combine the water, lemon juice, and sugar over medium heat and cook, swirling the pan occasionally, for 3 to 4 minutes, until the sugar dissolves.

2. Add the apples and cook for 6 to 8 minutes, until the apples are tender but not soft. Add the apricots and cook until just tender, about 2 minutes.

3. Serve warm or at room temperature garnished with a strip of lemon zest.

5 Family Feasts

oliday meals are the events that punctuate the year, mark the changes of seasons, remind us what life should be about. In our house these are sprawling family affairs with relatives and friends and their kids. Kids are a vital part of the affair; they put us on our best behavior and reconnect us to our youth.

Most of the dishes in the following menus can be adjusted easily for babies as young as six months. Until they are about eighteen months, they will probably eat only a small portion of one or two dishes.

Thanksgiving | 96

Christmas | 108

Easter | 122

Passover | 129

Fourth of July | 140

Thanksgiving

roasted young turkey with pumpkin risotto stuffing | 99

string beans with garlic croutons and bacon | 101

caramel cranberry sauce | 102

super mashed potatoes | 104

apple ginger pie with vanilla sauce and spiced cream | 105

Thanksgiving is our favorite holiday.
It's a harvest feast, where the bounty of the season is celebrated
at the table with friends and family. And it doesn't involve
frenzied gift shopping.

Some of these dishes can be completely or
partially prepared in advance, so that you don't have to spend
the entire holiday in the kitchen.

Two days ahead:
make the cranberry sauce and prepare the pie dough.

One day ahead:
make the vanilla sauce; cook the beans; make the garlic croutons;
prepare the pumpkin for the risotto; bake the pie.

The day of the meal:
put the turkey in the oven; peel and quarter the potatoes
and place in a bowl of water until ready to cook; make the spiced
cream; start cooking the potatoes ½ hour before the turkey is done;
start the risotto; when the risotto is done, cover it and place it
in the oven with the turkey and turn off the oven; mash the potatoes;
and finish the beans.

roasted young turkey with pumpkin risotto stuffing

Risotto, which can be made with just about anything, makes an unusual but tasty stuffing, especially when made with pumpkin, which gives it a brilliant yellow color. We decided not to have pumpkin in its traditional role as pie for dessert, and have worked it into the menu here. Since the risotto would have to cook for too long in the turkey, it is prepared while the turkey is roasting, so it is not a stuffing in the true sense. It makes a great complement to the turkey, however. Use canned pumpkin purée only as a last resort.

NOTES ▶ For babies nine to twelve months old, remove about ½ cup of the risotto from the pan before seasoning and adding the cheese. Mash it, adding a little chicken broth if necessary. Make sure that the turkey is cut into small enough pieces and serve only to children a year and older.

Serves **10 to 12**

TURKEY

1 (10- to 12-pound) young
    free-range turkey

Sea salt and freshly ground
    black pepper

Extra virgin olive oil, for
    rubbing the turkey

PUMPKIN RISOTTO
STUFFING

1 (1-pound) fresh pumpkin,
    peeled, seeded, and cut in
    1-inch cubes, or 1⅓ cups
    canned, unsweetened
    pumpkin purée

7½ cups low-sodium chicken
    broth

10 tablespoons unsalted
    butter, at room
    temperature

⅓ cup finely minced onion

1 cup small button
    mushrooms

PUMPKIN RISOTTO STUFFING, continued

2 cups Arborio rice

1½ teaspoons finely minced fresh sage

Sea salt and freshly ground black pepper

½ cup freshly grated Parmesan cheese

TO SERVE

Fresh cranberries

Rosemary sprigs

1. To prepare the turkey, preheat the oven to 325°F. Remove the giblets from the turkey's cavities, rinse well, and pat dry with paper towels. Season the cavities with salt and pepper. Rub the exterior with olive oil and season with salt and pepper. Place the turkey breast side down in a large roasting pan.

2. Roast for 1½ to 2 hours, until the skin is golden brown. Turn the turkey over and continue roasting for another 2 hours.

3. While the turkey is roasting, prepare the pumpkin risotto. In a large covered pan, boil the fresh pumpkin in 1 cup lightly salted water for about 10 minutes,

(continued on page 100)

CONTINUED FROM PAGE 99

until the pumpkin is tender and can be pierced easily with the tip of a knife. Transfer the pumpkin with ½ cup of its cooking liquid to a blender or food processor fitted with a steel blade and purée. Set aside. If you are using canned pumpkin purée, omit this step.

4. Bring the chicken broth to a steady simmer in a large saucepan.

5. In a large heavy-bottomed pan over medium heat, melt 4 tablespoons of the butter. Add the onion and cook for 6 to 8 minutes, until translucent. Add the mushrooms and cook for 3 minutes. Add the rice and, using a wooden spoon, stir for 1 to 2 minutes, until all the grains are coated. Add the broth ½ cup at a time, stirring frequently. When the rice has almost absorbed the broth, add the next ½ cup. Continue adding more broth and stirring, reserving ½ cup of broth for the finish.

6. When the rice is tender but still firm and 7 cups of the broth of been added and absorbed, mix in the reserved ½ cup broth, the pumpkin purée, sage, and salt and pepper. Add the cheese and the remaining 6 tablespoons of butter. Remove from heat and cover to keep warm. (See menu plan on page 96.)

7. When the turkey has roasted for 3½ to 4 hours, check for doneness by jiggling the leg; if it moves easily, it's done. You can also insert a meat thermometer in the breast. It should register 165°F. Remove the turkey from the oven and let it rest 15 minutes before carving.

8. To serve, place the turkey on a bed of fresh cranberries and sprigs of rosemary on a serving platter. Place the risotto in a serving dish.

string beans with garlic croutons and bacon

Ciabatta, a crusty Italian bread, adds a good crunch to this traditional Thanksgiving dish. French bread also will work.

NOTES

Omit the bacon and croutons, and purée just the beans for babies six to nine months old; mash them for babies ten to twelve months old. Depending on their ability to chew, babies from one to three years old can handle cut up beans and bacon. Break up the croutons—they can present a choking hazard.

Serves 10 to 12

3 pounds green beans, trimmed

½ pound apple-smoked bacon, cut into small dice

1 clove garlic, minced

½ pound ciabatta bread, cut into ½-inch cubes

1. Bring a large saucepan of lightly salted water to a boil. Add the beans and cook for 4 to 5 minutes, until crisp-tender. Immediately drain the beans and refresh in ice water. When cool, drain the beans and set aside.

2. In a large skillet, sauté the bacon and garlic over medium heat for about 5 minutes, stirring constantly. Add the bread cubes and sauté for about 5 minutes, stirring, until crisp. Add the beans and sauté for 3 to 5 minutes, until heated through.

3. Serve warm.

caramel cranberry sauce

Deglazing with cream lightens the texture of the sauce.

| NOTES | Mash this well for babies nine months to three years old; whole berries can present a choking hazard for children under three. |

Makes 4 cups

2 cups granulated sugar

⅔ cup water

⅔ cup heavy whipping cream

2 pounds fresh cranberries, washed, dried, and any bad berries discarded

Zest of two lemons, cut into strips

1. Combine the sugar and water in a heavy-bottomed saucepan. Dissolve the sugar in the water over medium heat until the liquid is completely clear. Increase the heat to high and cook (without stirring) until the caramel is a golden amber color.

2. Remove the caramel from the heat and slowly whisk in the cream, a few tablespoons at a time. The mixture will bubble as you add the cream.

3. Add the cranberries to the caramel and cook over low heat until tender. Stir in the lemon zest. Serve at room temperature.

super mashed potatoes

This is one of my signature dishes and a holiday dish that almost the whole family can enjoy—it's too rich for babies younger than nine months old.

Serves 10 to 12

4 pounds Yukon gold potatoes, peeled and quartered

2 cups milk or cream, heated

10 tablespoons unsalted butter, at room temperature, cut into cubes

½ cup plain yogurt

Salt and freshly ground black pepper

1. In a large, heavy-bottomed saucepan, bring lightly salted water to a boil and carefully drop in the potatoes. Decrease the heat and cook for about 30 minutes, until the potatoes are tender and easily pierced with the tip of a knife.

2. Drain immediately and press the potatoes through a potato ricer.

3. Return the riced potatoes to the saucepan. Beat in the milk until smooth. Add the butter and beat until completely melted. Over low heat, stir in the yogurt.

4. Season with salt and pepper. Serve warm.

apple ginger pie with vanilla sauce and spiced cream

Ginger adds a little bite to an otherwise traditional apple pie. For a large group, you may want to make two pies or have an extra dessert.

| NOTES | This is not suitable for babies younger than eighteen months. At eighteen months, they can have a small portion cut into little pieces. |

Serves 10

PIE CRUST

4 cups all-purpose flour

⅓ cup sugar

1 teaspoon salt

¾ cup unsalted butter, chilled and cut into cubes

2 egg yolks

6 tablespoons water

¼ cup milk

2 tablespoons coarse raw sugar

FILLING

3 pounds Golden Delicious apples, peeled, cored, and cut into ½-inch slices

1 cup sugar

¼ cup all-purpose flour

3 tablespoons minced crystallized ginger

¼ teaspoon ground cinnamon

TO SERVE

Vanilla Sauce (recipe follows)

Spiced Cream (recipe follows)

1. Preheat the oven to 375°F.

2. To prepare the crust, mix the flour, sugar, salt, and butter in a food processor fitted with a steel blade. Mix until a coarse meal forms. Add the egg yolks and pulse three or four times. Continue to mix, adding the water 1 tablespoon at a time, pausing to scrape down the sides of the bowl, until a ball forms. Be careful not to overmix or the dough will be tough. The dough can also be mixed by hand.

3. Turn the dough out onto a floured surface. Divide in half. Form each half into a ball and flatten into a disk. Wrap each disk tightly in plastic wrap and refrigerate for at least 1 hour. This can be done 3 days ahead.

4. To prepare the filling, mix the apples, sugar, flour, ginger, and cinnamon in a bowl. Allow to sit for an hour.

5. Place one of the dough disks on a floured surface. Roll out to a thickness of ¼ inch and 1 inch larger in diameter than the pie dish. Loosely fold the dough into quarters and carefully place it into the pie dish. Press it into the bottom and sides, leaving the excess dough hanging over the edge. Drain the filling mixture and toss several times. Mound into the pie dish. Roll out the dough for the top crust in the same manner as the bottom crust. Place it over the filling. Trim both crusts to about ½ inch and crimp the edges together decoratively. Cut five slashes in the top, radiating from the center. Brush the top with milk and sprinkle with the raw sugar. *(continued on page 106)*

CONTINUED FROM PAGE 105

6. Bake for about 1 hour, until golden brown. Cool on a metal rack for about 20 minutes.

7. Drizzle each serving with Vanilla Sauce and place a dollop of Spiced Cream on the side.

vanilla sauce

This can be made a day ahead and refrigerated. Remove the sauce from the refrigerator just before serving.

NOTES	The apple pie is sweet enough for children under three without the addition of vanilla sauce or spiced cream.

Makes 2½ cups

1 cup heavy cream

1½ cups whole milk

1 teaspoon vanilla extract
   (Tahitian recommended)

6 egg yolks

⅓ cup sugar

1. In a medium saucepan, combine the cream and milk and bring to a boil. Stir in the vanilla.

2. With the whisk attachment, beat the egg yolks and sugar in the bowl of a stand mixer until pale yellow and thick.

3. Pour the hot cream mixture into the egg yolk mixture and whisk together.

4. Return the mixture to the saucepan and stir with a wooden spoon over low heat. Heat only until the mixture thickens and coats the spoon. Do not allow it to simmer or boil.

5. Once it is thickened, remove the mixture from the heat and set the pan in a bowl of ice water. Stir it as it cools.

6. Strain the mixture through a fine-mesh strainer. Serve at room temperature. The sauce can be prepared a day ahead. Transfer it to a bowl, lay a piece of wax paper on the surface, and refrigerate.

spiced cream

Makes 4 cups

4 cups heavy cream

½ cup confectioners' sugar

½ teaspoon ground
   cinnamon

½ teaspoon ground nutmeg

1. In the large bowl of an electric mixer, beat the cream and sugar at high speed for about 3 minutes. Add the cinnamon and nutmeg and continue beating until the cream thickens and forms stiff peaks.

2. Serve immediately. This can also be made a day in advance and refrigerated.

Christmas

butternut squash soup with wild mushroom crouton | 111

green salad with pomegranate, apples, pecans, and oranges
with champagne vinaigrette | 112

salt-crusted beef rib roast | 114

popovers | 115

mashed turnips | 116

creamed cipollini onions and spinach | 117

roasted large-dice root vegetables | 119

orange almond cake with orange syrup and crème fraîche | 120

In the kitchen we pull out all the stops for Christmas.
This is a true feast and even when the boys were very little
they knew something special was going on.

Although the size and complexity of the menu
may appear daunting, several of the dishes can be made or prepped in
advance, making the day of the meal less hectic.

Three days ahead:
caramelize the pecans.

One day ahead:
bake the cake; prepare the orange syrup and purchase the
crème fraîche; make the soup and the vinaigrette.

The day of the meal:
peel and chop the root vegetables and the turnips; remove the beef
from the refrigerator an hour before you plan to cook it; mince the
shallot and chop the mushrooms for the soup; prepare the ingredients
for the salad, then cover and refrigerate them; put the root vegetables
in the oven about 45 minutes before you plan to put the beef
in the oven; wash and stem the spinach and peel the cipollini onions;
remove the root vegetables from the oven when they are done and
cover them with aluminum foil to keep warm; put the beef in the oven;
while the beef is cooking, boil the turnips and prepare the
onions and the spinach, timing both to finish just as the beef is done;
while the beef is resting, bake the popovers, mash the turnips, reheat
the soup, sauté the mushrooms, and toast the croutons;
just before serving, combine the salad ingredients and toss with the
vinaigrette or serve on the side.

butternut squash soup with wild mushroom crouton

The savory-sweet flavor of the squash provides a satisfying contrast with the earthy taste of the mushrooms and the crunch of the crouton. Black trumpet, chanterelle, shiitake, and cèpe mushrooms are good choices for the crouton.

| NOTES | ▶ For babies six months to one year old, purée some of the cooked flesh from the squash moistened with chicken stock. Reserve the crouton for children three years and older. |

Serves 6

SOUP

3 pounds butternut squash, halved and seeded

6 to 7 tablespoons unsalted butter

Sea salt and freshly ground black pepper

1 large onion, finely chopped

1 large carrot, peeled and cut into ½-inch slices

2 celery stalks, trimmed and cut into ½-inch slices

1 cup low-sodium chicken broth, plus extra for purée

WILD MUSHROOM CROUTONS

2 tablespoons unsalted butter

1 tablespoon finely minced shallot

3 ounces wild mushrooms, finely chopped

6 slices (½-inch thick) ciabatta bread

Extra virgin olive oil, for brushing bread

6 sprigs fresh thyme

1. Preheat the oven to 375°F.

2. To prepare the soup, place the squash halves on a sheet pan cut side up. Place 1 tablespoon of butter in each cavity and season with salt and pepper. Cover the pan with aluminum foil and roast for about 30 to 45 minutes, until the squash is tender and easily pierced with the tip of a knife. Remove from the oven and set aside to cool. Leave the oven on.

3. In a large pot, melt 4 tablespoons of the butter over medium-high heat. Add the onion, carrot, and celery and sauté for about 5 minutes. Add the broth and cook over medium heat for about 10 minutes more, until the vegetables are tender. Remove the pan from the heat and let cool. Transfer the mixture to a food processor fitted with a steel blade and purée until smooth.

4. Scrape the flesh from the squash and add to the food processor. Purée until smooth, adding more broth as needed. Taste and adjust seasonings.

5. To prepare the crouton, melt the butter in a sauté pan over medium heat. Add the shallot and sauté for 3 minutes, until the shallot is translucent. Add the mushrooms and sauté for another 4 minutes, until tender.

6. Lightly brush the slices of bread on both sides with oil and place on a baking sheet. Bake for 5 to 7 minutes,

(continued on page 112)

Family Feasts

CONTINUED FROM PAGE 111

then turn over and, watching closely, bake 2 to 3 minutes until golden. Remove from the oven and set aside.

7. To serve, reheat the soup until just bubbling and pour into individual bowls. Place a table-spoon of the mushroom mixture on one end of each crouton, and position on the rim of each soup plate. Garnish the soup with a small sprig of fresh thyme.

green salad with pomegranate, apples, pecans, and oranges with champagne vinaigrette

Full of bright contrasting flavors and textures, this refreshing salad wakes up the palate for what follows. If you're not serving this to children, add a tablespoon of Champagne to the dressing to add a little frisson.

NOTES The texture of salad is usually not attractive to babies. If your baby is eighteen months or older and you want to offer a taste, cut the greens, the fruit, and the celery into small pieces and moisten with the dress-ing. Omit the pecans and pomegranate seeds if you are serving the salad to children under three.

Serves 6

CARAMELIZED PECANS

¾ cup pecans

1 cup confectioners' sugar

Vegetable shortening, for frying

CHAMPAGNE VINAIGRETTE

1 tablespoon Champagne vinegar or white balsamic vinegar

Sea salt and freshly ground black pepper

¼ cup extra virgin olive oil

CHAMPAGNE VINAIGRETTE, continued

1 teaspoon Dijon mustard

1 tablespoon Champagne (optional)

GREEN SALAD

18 ounces mixed greens, washed, dried, and torn into bite-size pieces

Seeds of 1 large pomegranate

3 Lady apples, peeled and thinly sliced

3 Valencia oranges, peeled and membrane removed, separated into segments

1 celery stalk, trimmed and sliced into thin strips

christmas

1. To prepare the pecans, bring a pot of water to a boil. Add the pecans. When the water returns to a boil, remove the pecans with a slotted spoon. Drain and spread them on a sheet pan to cool for 2 minutes. While still slightly moist, coat them generously with the confectioners' sugar.

2. Melt enough shortening to equal a depth of at least 1 inch in a heavy sauté pan over medium-high heat. When the oil registers 350°F on a candy thermometer, carefully add the coated pecans in batches. Fry for about 5 minutes, until they are a rich, dark brown. Remove each batch with a slotted spoon and place on a cooling rack. These can be made ahead and stored for 3 days in an airtight container.

3. To prepare the vinaigrette, whisk together the vinegar, salt, and pepper. Add the oil and mustard, continuing to whisk until the ingredients have emulsified. If serving to adults, whisk in the Champagne.

4. To prepare the salad, in a large serving bowl, toss the greens with the pomegranate seeds. Add the apples, oranges, celery, and pecans, and toss.

5. Pour the vinaigrette over the salad just before serving. The vinaigrette may also be served on the side.

salt-crusted beef rib roast

The salt crust seals in the juices in the meat, with juicy, flavorful results.

| NOTES | The salt and egg white make this unsuitable for babies younger than one year old. For older babies, cut the meat up into tiny pieces. |

Serves 6

1 (4-rib) roast, about
    6 pounds, trimmed of
    most excess fat

½ cup egg whites

Coarse sea salt, for coating

Freshly ground black pepper

1. At least 1 hour before starting to cook, remove the meat from the refrigerator to reach room temperature.

2. Preheat the oven to 450°F.

3. Generously coat the meat with the egg whites, cover with the salt, and season with the pepper.

4. Place the meat bone side down in a large roasting pan. Roast for 15 minutes. Turn the oven temperature down to 350°F and roast for 1 hour. Check the roast in several places with a meat thermometer. If it registers at least 125°F in each spot, the meat is rare. If you want it more well-done, return the roast to the oven for another 5 to 10 minutes and check again. Don't let the meat reach 155°F or it will be overdone.

5. Cover the roast with aluminum foil and let rest for about ½ hour, while you prepare the popovers. To serve, cut into ½-inch slices.

popovers

The popovers replace Yorkshire pudding as an accompaniment to the beef roast in this English-style dish.

| NOTES | ▶ Tear the popovers into little pieces for babies one to two years old. |

Makes about 1 dozen

1 cup all-purpose flour

¼ teaspoon sea salt

1 cup whole milk

3 large eggs

1 tablespoon unsalted butter, melted

Pinch of fresh thyme

1. Preheat the oven to 450°F. Grease a popover tin with melted butter and place in the oven to heat.

2. In a medium bowl, mix the flour and salt.

3. In a separate bowl, whisk together the milk, eggs, and butter. Pour into the flour mixture. Add the thyme and whisk until just blended.

4. Remove the heated pan from the oven and carefully fill each cup halfway with the batter. Place in the oven and lower the heat to 350°F. Bake for 15 to 20 minutes. The tops should be browned, but don't open the oven to check until they have baked for at least 15 minutes. They fall easily.

5. Serve hot from the oven.

mashed turnips

Turnips have a sweet, delicate flavor and can be used as a good alternative to mashed potatoes. Chooose white or purple-tinged ones, no larger that two inches in diameter.

NOTES ▶ **Mashed turnips can be served to babies nine months and older.**

Serves 6

3 pounds turnips, peeled and cut into chunks

3 tablespoons unsalted butter, at room temperature

½ cup whole milk, heated

Sea salt and freshly ground black pepper

1. Bring a large pot of lightly salted water to a boil. Add the turnips and cook for 15 to 20 minutes, until tender. Drain.

2. Combine the turnips with the butter and milk in a food processor fitted with a steel blade, and purée.

3. Season with salt and pepper and serve with the beef.

creamed cipollini onions and spinach

This little onion, actually a bulb of the grape hyacinth, can be found in Italian and specialty markets in the fall.

| NOTES | For babies eighteen months and older, purée or mash with the liquid, depending on your baby's ability to chew. |

Serves 6

¼ cup extra virgin olive oil

1½ pounds cipollini onions, peeled

8 ounces spinach, rinsed and stemmed

½ cup heavy cream

Sea salt and freshly ground black pepper

1. In a large heavy pan, heat the oil over medium heat for 1 minute. Add the onions, cover, and cook for 20 to 30 minutes, until tender.

2. In a large sauté pan over medium-high heat, cook the spinach with just the water that clings to its leaves for 2 to 3 minutes, until it is bright green and tender. Refresh the spinach in iced water. When cool, drain it and remove the excess water by squeezing it with your hands.

3. When the onions are tender, decrease the heat to medium, add the cream, and cook for 1 to 2 minutes, until bubbling. Add the spinach and cook for 2 to 3 minutes, until it's warm and the sauce has thickened slightly.

4. Season with salt and pepper and serve.

roasted large-dice root vegetables

Scarlet beets and orange carrots make this an attractive dish for a holiday table, and it's the ideal winter comfort food.

| NOTES | The presence of nitrates in some root vegetables, especially beets, make this unsuitable for babies younger than nine months. For babies nine to eighteen months old, pick out the parsnips, rutabagas, and carrots, and purée with a little liquid. For older babies, chop the vegetables into smaller pieces. |

Serves 6

2 celery roots, peeled and cut
  into large dice

3 parsnips, peeled and cut
  into large dice

3 rutabagas, peeled and cut
  into large dice

6 carrots, peeled and cut into
  large dice

3 onions, cut into large dice

Extra virgin olive oil, for
  coating

Sea salt and freshly ground
  black pepper

6 cloves garlic, minced

Leaves of 1 sprig fresh thyme

6 red beets, peeled and cut
  into large dice

1 tablespoon aged balsamic
  vinegar

1. Preheat the oven to 375°F.

2. Combine the celery roots, parsnips, rutabagas, carrots, and onions in a large shallow roasting pan. Coat with olive oil, salt, pepper, garlic, and some of the thyme. Roast for 45 to 55 minutes, until the vegetables are tender and easily pierced with the tip of a knife.

3. Coat the beets with olive oil, salt, pepper, and thyme, and roast in a separate pan but at the same time as the other vegetables for about 45 minutes, until tender. Put both pans on the middle rack if they will fit. If not, use the racks just above and below the middle, and switch positions after about 35 minutes.

4. Remove the pans from the oven and mix the beets into the other vegetables. Return to the oven and roast for another 5 minutes.

5. Toss with the balsamic vinegar. Season with salt and pepper. Serve immediately.

orange almond cake with orange syrup and crème fraîche

The contrast of tart and sweet is the attraction of this cake. Crème fraîche can be purchased in most grocery and health food stores.

NOTES	**Babies one year old and up without allergies to nuts can enjoy a little bite of cake with a dab of crème fraîche. Omit the orange syrup for children under three. The cake is sweet enough.**

Serves 8 to 10

ORANGE ALMOND CAKE

3 Valencia oranges

12 ounces whole blanched
   almonds

1½ teaspoons baking powder

7 large eggs

1⅔ cups sugar

ORANGE SYRUP

20 kumquats, halved

Juice of 6 Valencia oranges

Juice of 1 lemon

¾ cup sugar

½ cup water

TO SERVE

Confectioners' sugar, for
   dusting

Crème fraîche, for garnish

1. Preheat the oven to 350°F. Grease a 10-inch spring-form pan and line the bottom with parchment paper.

2. To prepare the cake, bring a large pot of water to a rapid boil. Add the oranges and cook for 10 to15 minutes, until soft. Set aside to cool, then purée unpeeled in a food processor fitted with a steel blade.

3. Process the almonds in a food processor to a medium-fine texture and combine with the baking powder.

4. In the bowl of a stand mixer fitted with a whisk attachment, beat the eggs and sugar on high speed until they are thick and pale. Using a large rubber spatula, gently fold in the puréed orange and the almond mixture by hand.

5. Pour the batter into the prepared pan and bake for 1 hour, or until the cake is firm to the touch. Let the cake cool in the pan for 30 minutes, and then release it upside down onto a rack and allow to cool completely.

6. To make the syrup, combine the kumquats, orange juice, lemon juice, sugar, and water in a saucepan and bring to a boil. Decrease the heat to a simmer and cook for about 20 minutes (without stirring), until the mixture is thick and syrupy.

7. To serve, place the cake on a platter and sift confectioners' sugar evenly over the top. Serve the sauce and crème fraîche in bowls on the side.

Easter

roasted leg of lamb with spring vegetables and shiitake mushrooms | 123

roasted herbed new potatoes | 125

asparagus and eight-minute egg with champagne vinaigrette | 126

panna cotta with balsamic marinated strawberries | 128

Easter signals that nature is waking up and soon we'll have fresh spring produce. We celebrate Easter in a traditional manner, with a boisterous Easter egg hunt and lamb for dinner.

This is not a challenging menu
and some of the dishes can be prepped in advance.

One day ahead:
make the panna cotta and marinate the strawberries;
prepare the vinaigrette.

The day of the meal:
blanch the garlic for the lamb; prepare the ingredients for the spring vegetables; cut the potatoes; boil the eggs and cut the asparagus; while the lamb is roasting, cook the spring vegetables and prepare the potatoes for roasting; while the lamb is resting, roast the potatoes and cook the asparagus.

roasted leg of lamb with spring vegetables and shiitake mushrooms

NOTES ▷ Purée the lamb with some snap peas and chicken stock for babies nine to eighteen months. Mash up the vegetables except the artichokes with the lamb for babies eighteen months to three years.

Serves 6 to 8

LEG OF LAMB

1 leg of lamb, bone-in,
    5 to 6 pounds, excess fat
    trimmed

6 tablespoons plus 1 teaspoon
    extra virgin olive oil

Leaves of 2 sprigs fresh thyme

Sea salt and freshly ground
    black pepper

8 cloves garlic

¼ cup hot water

SPRING VEGETABLES

2 tablespoons unsalted butter

1½ pounds pearl onions,
    peeled

1 tablespoon sugar

½ cup low-sodium chicken
    broth

1 pound sugar snap peas,
    trimmed

1 pound green beans,
    trimmed

4 artichokes

¼ cup lemon juice

3 tablespoons extra virgin
    olive oil

1 tablespoon thinly sliced
    shallot

SPRING VEGETABLES, continued

5 garlic cloves, peeled and minced

Sea salt and freshly ground black pepper

1 pound shiitake mushrooms, stems removed and caps
    cut into ½-inch strips

Sprigs of thyme, for garnish

1. Preheat the oven to 450°F.

2. Rub the lamb with the 6 tablespoons oil and the
   thyme. Season with salt and pepper and place it in a
   roasting pan.

3. Roast for 15 minutes. Decrease the heat to 350°F and
   roast for 30 to 40 minutes longer.

4. Meanwhile, bring a small pan of water to a boil.
   Add the garlic and blanch for 2 minutes. Repeat this
   process three times with fresh water. Remove the
   garlic and set aside.

5. Remove the pan from the oven and scatter the garlic
   over the lamb. Return to the oven and continue roasting for 15 to 20 minutes. Using a meat thermometer,
   check the lamb in several places after about 1 hour of
   roasting. If it registers 125°F it is rare; at 135°F it is
   medium-rare.

6. Remove the lamb from the oven and let it rest for
   30 minutes. Place it on a serving dish. Over medium-
   high heat, deglaze the roasting pan with the meat
   juices and the ¼ cup hot water, scraping up the brown
   bits from the bottom of the pan. Pour the sauce
   through a fine-mesh sieve into a serving bowl. Stir
   in the 1 teaspoon oil. *(continued on page 124)*

7. To prepare the onions, melt the butter in a large sauté pan over medium-high heat. Add the onions and cook for 1 minute. Sprinkle evenly with the sugar, decrease the heat to medium, and cook for about 10 minutes, turning the onions with a wooden spoon until glazed and golden brown on both sides. Add the broth and cook, stirring to scrape up any bits stuck to the bottom, until the onions are tender, another 5 to 10 minutes. This can be made 1 day in advance and refrigerated when cool.

8. To prepare the peas, bring a large pan of lightly salted water to a boil. Add the peas, bring back to a boil, and cook for 2 to 3 minutes, until the peas are bright green. Remove them and refresh in ice water. Drain. The peas can be prepared a day ahead and stored in the refrigerator.

9. To prepare the beans, fill the same pot with lightly salted water and bring to a boil. Add the beans and cook for 4 to 6 minutes, until the beans are bright green. Remove them and refresh in ice water. When cool, drain and set aside. The beans can be prepared a day ahead and stored in the refrigerator.

10. To prepare the artichokes, first peel off the tough outer leaves. Trim around the base and cut the top leaves as close as possible to the artichoke heart without removing any flesh. Remove the fuzzy center with your fingers and, with a spoon, lightly scrape the cavity of the heart. Soak in about 4 cups of water with ¼ cup lemon juice. When you are ready to cook, drain the artichokes and quarter them.

11. Heat the oil in a large sauté pan over medium-high heat for 1 minute. Add the shallots and garlic, and sauté for 1 minute. Add the artichokes and season with salt and pepper. Cover and cook, turning the artichokes occasionally with kitchen tongs to brown on all sides. After 10 minutes, test for tenderness with a knife. They should pierce easily.

12. Increase the heat to high, add the mushrooms, and sauté for 5 minutes. The artichokes should have a nice golden brown color.

13. Add the onions with their liquid to the artichoke-mushroom mixture and cook for 2 minutes. Add the sugar snap peas and string beans for 1 to 2 minutes, just to heat. Do not overcook or the peas will turn brown.

14. To serve, slice the lamb into ½-inch pieces and place in the center of a serving platter. Arrange the spring vegetables around it. Garnish with sprigs of fresh thyme. Pass the sauce on the side.

roasted herbed new potatoes

NOTES ▶ For babies nine months to one year old, purée a few slices of potato with a little water; mash or cut them into small pieces for toddlers.

Serves 6

3 pounds new potatoes,
  halved lengthwise

¼ cup extra virgin olive oil

1 clove garlic, minced

1 tablespoon fresh rosemary

Sea salt and freshly ground
  black pepper

Pinch of fresh thyme leaves

1 tablespoon minced fresh
  oregano leaves

1. Preheat the oven to 350°F.

2. Arrange the potatoes in a single layer in a large oven-proof baking dish and toss to coat with the oil, garlic, and rosemary. Season with salt and pepper.

3. Roast, uncovered, for 20 to 25 minutes. Remove the pan from the oven and add the thyme and oregano, turning the potatoes with a wooden spatula. Continue roasting for another 10 minutes, until the potatoes are tender and easily pierced with the tip of a knife.

4. Serve immediately or at room temperature.

asparagus and eight-minute egg with champagne vinaigrette

Choose very fresh asparagus, similar in size so that they cook at the same rate.

NOTES The hard-cooked egg yolk can be puréed with some asparagus and enough water or chicken broth to make it smooth for babies nine months to one year old. For babies one year and older, mash the asparagus with both the yolk and egg white.

Serves 6

36 stalks asparagus, medium to large, ends trimmed

6 large eggs

CHAMPAGNE VINAIGRETTE

1½ tablespoons champagne vinegar

Pinch of sea salt

1 cup extra virgin olive oil

1 tablespoon minced shallot

Freshly ground black pepper

1 bunch chives, minced, for garnish (optional)

1. Bring a large pan of salted water to a boil, add the asparagus, and blanch for 5 to 7 minutes, until just tender. Drain and immediately refresh in ice water. When the asparagus is cool, drain and set aside.

2. Pierce the eggs with a pin at the wide end and place in a medium saucepan with boiling water over high heat. Cook them for 8 minutes. Place in a bowl of cold water to cool.

3. To prepare the champagne vinaigrette, whisk the vinegar, salt, oil, shallot, and pepper in a small bowl.

4. On a cutting board, line up the asparagus at the tips and cut the stalks to the same length. Chop the stalks into smaller pieces for children three years and older.

5. To serve, arrange the asparagus on individual serving plates or a platter. Shell the eggs, cut into medium dice, and scatter over the asparagus. Drizzle 2 to 3 tablespoons of the vinaigrette over each serving. Sprinkle with chives.

panna cotta with balsamic marinated strawberries

A good balsamic vinegar, aged ten years or more, will boost the flavor of the strawberries and provide a satisfying contrast with the smooth sweetness of the "cooked cream."

> **NOTES** Everyone over the age of one can eat this. Purée or mash the berries without the vinegar for children younger than three years old.

Serves 8

3 cups heavy cream

1 cup whole milk

2 cups confectioners' sugar

1 vanilla bean

3 sheets leaf gelatin

1½ pounds strawberries, hulled and halved

5 tablespoons granulated sugar

5 teaspoons aged balsamic vinegar

1. In a large saucepan, combine the cream, milk, and confectioners' sugar. Slice the vanilla bean open lengthwise, scrape out the seeds, and add both the seeds and the pod to the cream mixture. Mix and bring to a boil over medium-high heat. Decrease the heat and simmer for about 7 minutes.

2. Remove the pan from the heat and add the gelatin, stirring with a wooden spoon until dissolved.

3. Remove the vanilla bean and strain the mixture through a fine-mesh sieve. Pour into individual serving dishes and chill for at least 3 hours.

4. In a bowl, mix the strawberries, granulated sugar, and vinegar, making sure the berries are completely coated. Let marinate for 30 minutes, stirring occasionally.

5. Serve the panna cotta chilled and pass the strawberries on the side.

Passover

matzo ball soup | 131

braised veal shank with spring vegetables | 132

spinach with pine nuts | 136

flourless chocolate hazelnut cake | 138

Although Passover meals are prepared
according to strict dietary guidelines, that doesn't prevent the dishes
from being delicious for the entire family.

Time spent in the kitchen can be lessened with
a few advance preparations.

One day ahead:
marinate the veal; prepare the chicken soup and the dough for
the matzo balls; bake the cake.

The day of meal:
prepare the ingredients for the spring vegetables; wash the spinach
and toast the pine nuts; put the veal in the oven; while it is cooking,
cook the spring vegetables; heat the chicken soup and cook the matzo
balls; when the lamb is done, sauté the spinach.

matzo ball soup

Everyone needs a bowl of chicken soup at some point. The chicken used to prepare this soup can be used later for salad or chicken pot pie.

<table>
<tr><td>NOTES</td><td>▶</td><td>**Purée or mash the matzo ball with the soup for babies one to three years old.**</td></tr>
</table>

Serves 8

CHICKEN SOUP

1 (4-pound) whole chicken

3 celery stalks, cut into 3-inch pieces

2 large onions, quartered

3 carrots, peeled and cut into 3-inch pieces

Bouquet garni (3 sprigs each of thyme, rosemary, marjoram, oregano, and tarragon tied together with kitchen twine)

4 cloves garlic

MATZO BALLS

2 cups finely ground matzo crackers

4 large eggs, slightly beaten

1 teaspoon kosher salt

2 tablespoons club soda

¼ cup vegetable oil

2 teaspoons finely minced flat-leaf parsley

1. Rinse the chicken under cold water and pat dry with paper towels.

2. To prepare the soup, combine the chicken, celery, onions, carrots, bouquet garni, and garlic in a heavy-bottomed pot with water to cover. Bring to a boil. Decrease the heat, cover, and cook for 1 hour, or until the juices run clear when the chicken is pierced in the thigh with a knife. Remove the chicken and set aside to cool. Strain the broth, discarding the vegetables, and skim off any excess fat. Strain the broth once more through a fine-mesh sieve and return to the pot.

3. While the soup is cooking, prepare the matzo balls. Thoroughly mix the matzo meal and eggs. Add the salt, club soda, oil, and parsley. Refrigerate for at least 30 minutes or overnight.

4. Set the broth over medium heat for about 10 minutes before adding the matzo balls.

5. With your hands, form the matzo mixture into balls about 2 inches in diameter and place in the heated broth. Cook for about 40 minutes over medium heat, until expanded and tender.

6. Serve immediately.

braised veal shank with spring vegetables

Braising is one of my favorite cooking techniques. The slow cooking produces wonderful flavor, and the meat becomes very tender.

NOTES ▶ Purée the veal with either the peas, carrots, or beans and chicken stock for babies twelve to eighteen months old. Mash up all of the vegetables with the veal for babies eighteen months to three years old.

Serves 8

VEAL SHANKS

8 (10- to 12-ounce) veal shanks

3 tablespoons extra virgin olive oil, plus extra for marinade

5 cloves garlic, minced

2 fresh sage leaves, minced

2 large carrots, peeled and cut into 1-inch cubes

2 celery stalks, trimmed and cut into 2-inch pieces

2 large onions, quartered

½ pound tomatoes, chopped

1 tablespoon tomato paste

6 cups veal or chicken broth

Sea salt and freshly ground black pepper

SPRING VEGETABLES

2 tablespoons unsalted butter

1½ pounds pearl onions, peeled

1 tablespoon sugar

½ cup low-sodium chicken broth

1 pound sugar snap peas, trimmed

1 pound green beans, trimmed

8 baby carrots, peeled

4 artichokes

¼ cup lemon juice

3 tablespoons extra virgin olive oil

1 tablespoon thinly sliced shallots

5 cloves garlic, minced

Sea salt and freshly ground black pepper

1 pound shiitake mushrooms, stems removed and caps cut into ½-inch strips

Sprigs of thyme, for garnish

1. To prepare the veal shanks, rub them with olive oil, garlic, and sage. Let marinate in the refrigerator for 1 day.

2. Preheat the oven to 375°F.

3. Heat the 3 tablespoons oil in a large ovenproof casserole over high heat. Add the shanks and cook for 10 minutes, turning to brown on all sides. Remove from the pan and set aside. Decrease the heat to medium. Add the carrots, celery, and onions, and cook for 5 minutes. Add the tomatoes and stir in the tomato paste, coating the vegetables. Cook for about 5 minutes, until nicely browned. Add 2 cups of the broth, stirring to scrape up any browned bits stuck to the bottom ot the pan. Return the veal shanks to the casserole and fill with enough additional broth to cover the shanks halfway. Bring to a boil. Cover the casserole and place in the oven. Bake for 30 minutes.

4. Remove the casserole from the oven and turn the shanks over, adding more broth if it is getting low. Decrease the heat to 350°F and continue roasting for 40 to 50 minutes, until the meat is very tender and about to fall off the bone.

5. Remove the meat, set aside, and keep warm. Strain the broth, discarding the vegetables. Strain again with a fine-mesh sieve and pour into a small saucepan. Cook the broth over high heat to reduce to about 1 cup. Season with salt and pepper.

6. To prepare the pearl onions, melt the butter in a large sauté pan over medium-high heat. Add the onions and cook for 1 minute. Sprinkle evenly with the sugar, decrease the heat to medium, and cook for about 10 minutes, turning the onions with a wooden spoon until glazed and golden brown on both sides. Add the ½ cup broth and cook for another 5 to 10 minutes, stirring to scrape up any bits stuck to the bottom of the pan, until the onions are tender. This can be made 1 day in advance and refrigerated when cool.

7. To prepare the peas, bring a large pan of lightly salted water to a boil. Add the peas, bring back to a boil, and cook for 2 to 3 minutes, until the peas are bright green. Remove and refresh in ice water. Drain. The peas can be prepared a day ahead and stored in the refrigerator.

8. To prepare the beans, fill the same pot with lightly salted water and bring to a boil. Add the beans and cook for 4 to 6 minutes, until the beans are bright green. Remove and refresh in ice water. When cool, drain and set aside.

9. To prepare the carrots, fill the same pot with lightly salted water and bring to a boil. Add the carrots and cook for 4 to 5 minutes, until the carrots are tender and easily pierced. Drain and set aside.

(continued on page 134)

Family Feasts

CONTINUED FROM PAGE 133

10. To prepare the artichokes, first peel off the tough outer leaves. Trim around the base and cut the top leaves as close as possible to the artichoke heart without removing any flesh. Remove the fuzzy center with your fingers and, with a spoon, lightly scrape the cavity of the heart. Soak in about 4 cups of water with ¼ cup lemon juice. When you are ready to cook, drain the artichokes and quarter them.

11. Heat the oil in a large sauté pan over medium-high heat for 1 minute. Add the shallots and garlic, and sauté for 1 minute. Add the artichokes and season with salt and pepper. Cover and cook, turning the artichokes occasionally with kitchen tongs to brown on all sides. After 10 minutes, test for tenderness with a knife. They should pierce easily.

12. Increase the heat to high, add the mushrooms, and sauté for 5 minutes. The artichokes should have a nice golden brown color. Add the onions with their liquid and the peas, beans, and carrots. Cook over medium heat for 2 to 3 minutes, just to heat. Do not overcook or the peas will turn brown.

13. To serve, place the veal in the center of a serving platter and arrange the spring vegetables around it. Garnish with the thyme.

spinach with pine nuts

NOTES

> Purée the sautéed spinach without the pine nuts and before you have seasoned it for babies nine to eighteen months; chop it into small pieces for older babies up to three years. Children two and older may also have pine nuts.

Serves 8

½ cup pine nuts

5 tablespoons extra virgin olive oil

1 clove garlic, minced

1 shallot, minced

3 pounds spinach, washed and stemmed

1 tablespoon freshly squeezed lemon juice

Pinch of ground nutmeg

Sea salt and freshly ground black pepper

1. Preheat the oven to 350°F.

2. Spread the pine nuts on a baking sheet and toast for 3 to 5 minutes, until lightly browned. Watch closely; they go from toasted to burned in a matter of seconds.

3. In a large sauté pan, heat 2 tablespoons of the oil over medium-high heat for 1 minute. Add the garlic and shallot and sauté for 1 minute. Add the spinach and sauté, turning constantly, for 1 minute, until wilted. Add the pine nuts, the remaining 3 tablespoons of oil, and lemon juice, tossing constantly for 1 minute. Season with the nutmeg and salt and pepper.

4. Transfer immediately to a serving dish and serve.

flourless chocolate hazelnut cake

Serve this warm with Vanilla Sauce (page 106) and Spiced Cream (page 107) or crème fraîche.

> **NOTES** — **Even though we love this cake and are tempted to offer them a taste, babies are not ready to handle chocolate until they are over two years old.**

Serves 12

2 cups hazelnuts

12 ounces semisweet chocolate chips

1¼ cups unsalted butter

8 eggs, separated

2⅓ cups confectioners' sugar, plus extra for dusting

Pinch of sea salt

1. Preheat the oven to 375°F. Lightly grease a 10-inch springform pan and line with parchment paper.

2. In a food processor, grind the hazelnuts into small pieces.

3. Combine the chocolate and butter in a heatproof bowl over a pot of simmering water. Make sure the base of the bowl doesn't touch the water. Stir occasionally until the butter and chocolate have melted. Set aside to cool.

4. While the chocolate is melting, beat the egg yolks with a whisk.

5. Transfer the chocolate mixture to the bowl of a stand mixer fitted with the paddle attachment. On low speed, slowly add the egg yolks. Stir in the hazelnuts.

6. Sift the confectioners' sugar into a bowl and mix into the chocolate mixture. The mixture will be stiff.

7. In a separate bowl of the mixer, using the whisk attachment, beat the egg whites and salt on high speed until stiff peaks form.

8. Carefully fold one-third of the egg whites into the chocolate mixture with a large rubber spatula. Repeat this process until all the egg whites have been folded in.

9. Pour the mixture into the prepared cake pan and bake for 45 minutes. The cake is done when a toothpick inserted into the center comes out with a light coating. The cake will be moist.

10. Transfer the cake to a cooling rack and let it sit for 20 minutes. Remove from the spring-form pan, and place on a rack to cool completely.

11. Just before serving, sift confectioner's sugar over the top of the cake.

Family Feasts

Fourth of July

barbecue chicken in a spicy marinade | 142

baby back pork ribs in a sweet marinade | 144

corn and tomato bread | 145

corn off the cob and heirloom tomatoes with grilled
   onions | 146

baked bean with apple-smoked bacon | 147

roasted yukon gold potato slices | 148

rich chocolate brownies with warm chocolate sauce | 150

lemon sponge cake with mixed summer berries | 151

The Fourth is another holiday that is really all about family, friends,
and food, and it's during summer, when most produce is at its peak.

A large buffet such as this requires some strategy and advance
preparation if you plan on having time to spend with your guests.

One day ahead:
bake the corn bread and the sponge cake;
bake the brownies and prepare the chocolate sauce; braise the ribs;
marinate the chicken; prepare the corn for the salad;
and put the beans in water to soak overnight.

The day of the buffet:
bake the beans (they bake for approximately three hours,
so coordinate with the cooking times for other dishes) mix the berries
for the cake; finish the salad; roast the potatoes—they can go into the
oven with the beans about one-half hour before the beans are done;
grill the ribs and the chicken; and finish the cake.

barbecue chicken in a spicy marinade

We like to use organic chickens both for the flavor and because they haven't been sub-jected to hormones. And these chiles are hot! Taste the marinade before using it to gauge the heat. Remember to wear rubber gloves when handling chiles and wash your hands thoroughly afterwards.

NOTES	Grill a piece of chicken without the marinade for babies a year and older. Cut the meat into tiny pieces.

Serves 8

SPICY MARINADE

12 cloves garlic, unpeeled

3 fresh chiles, such as
    jalapeño, habanero,
    or serrano

½ cup extra virgin olive oil,
    plus extra for brushing

1 cup freshly squeezed
    orange juice

¼ cup minced cilantro
    leaves

½ teaspoon sea salt

1 teaspoon ground turmeric

Sea salt and freshly ground
    black pepper

2 (2- to 3-pound) fresh whole
    organic chickens, quar-
    tered

1. Preheat the oven to 375°F. Place the garlic on a lightly oiled baking sheet and roast for 20 to 30 min-utes, until soft and easily pierced. When cool enough to handle, remove the peels and mince.

2. To prepare the marinade, halve the chiles lengthwise, remove the stems and seeds, and mince. Mix together with the garlic, oil, orange juice, cilantro, salt, turmeric, and salt and pepper in a large bowl.

3. Add the chicken to the marinade and refrigerate for 3 hours, turning twice. Remove the chicken from the marinade when you are ready to grill.

4. Prepare a fire in a charcoal grill. When the coals are hot, make a two-level fire by pushing some of the coals to one side. Sear the chicken over the hotter side, turning once, then move to the cooler side to finish cooking. Cover the white meat with a pan to retain moisture. If you are using a gas grill turn one burner to high and the other to medium. Preheat with the lid down. Sear the chicken on the hotter side, then move pieces to the cooler side, and grill, closing the lid until the chicken is fully browned and the juices run clear when the meat is pierced near the bone. Brush the chicken lightly with olive oil while it's being grilled to keep it moist. Depending on the size of the chicken, breasts will take 8 to 12 minutes, legs and thighs up to 15 minutes.

5. Arrange pieces on a serving platter and serve.

baby back pork ribs in a sweet marinade

The Fourth is one of the few occasions when we indulge in baby back pork ribs. They're delicious in this sweet marinade, and it is just once a year.

NOTES ▶ **Serve babies one to three years old the grilled chicken instead. For older children, cut the meat off the ribs.**

Serves 8

DRY RUB

5 tablespoons sea salt

¼ cup brown sugar

¼ cup sweet paprika

2 tablespoons chili powder

2 tablespoons ground cumin

2 tablespoons ground turmeric

1 tablespoon cayenne pepper

1 teaspoon freshly ground black pepper

6 to 8 pounds baby back pork ribs

MARINADE

½ cup red wine vinegar

1 cup honey

6 tablespoons minced garlic

5 tablespoons Dijon mustard

2 teaspoons cumin

2 teaspoons turmeric

2 teaspoons cinnamon

1. To prepare the dry rub, mix the salt, sugar, paprika, chili powder, cumin, turmeric, cayenne, and black pepper in a bowl.

2. Preheat the oven to 350°F. The ribs must be precooked before grilling. Coat the ribs generously on all sides with the rub and place them on a baking sheet containing ½ inch of water. Lay them flat and cover with aluminum foil.

3. Place in the oven and braise for 30 to 40 minutes, until tender. The ribs can be braised the day before and refrigerated. They can go straight from the refrigerator to the grill.

4. While the ribs are cooking, prepare the marinade. Combine the vinegar, honey, garlic, mustard, cumin, turmeric, and cinnamon in a small saucepan and cook over low heat for about 10 minutes.

5. In preparation for grilling, soak wood chunks in cold water for 1 hour and drain or place wood chips on an 18-inch square of aluminum foil, seal to make a packet, and pierce holes to allow smoke to escape.

6. Light about forty charcoal briquettes. Shove some of the coals to one side of the grill, 2 to 3 briquettes high. When the coals are ashed over, lay the wood chunks or the prepared packet on top. Replace the grate and open the vents. Let the grill heat for 5 minutes.

7. Place the ribs on the hotter side of the grill and cook for 2 to 3 minutes on each side, then move them to the cooler side and cook for 2 to 3 minutes on each

side. These times are approximate; grilling time will depend on how hot your grill is, so watch carefully. Brush with the marinade after each turn and grill until the meat starts to pull away from the bone.

8. Arrange on a platter and serve immediately.

corn and tomato bread

Whole corn kernels and chunks of roasted tomato add a little surprise and texture to the usual suspect.

| NOTES | The whole corn kernels in the bread can be a choking hazard, so don't serve this to children younger than three years old. The bread can also be made without the corn kernels for children under three. |

Serves 8

3 large ears fresh corn, shucked

1¾ cups yellow cornmeal

1 cup all-purpose flour

½ cup sugar

1 teaspoon baking powder

1 teaspoon sea salt

1 teaspoon baking soda

1 large egg

2¼ cups buttermilk

¼ cup diced and drained fire-roasted tomatoes, (Muir Glen fire-roasted tomatoes are recommended)

1. Preheat the oven to 400°F. Lightly coat an 8-inch square baking pan with canola oil.

2. Bring a large pot of lightly salted water to a boil, add the corn, and cook for 5 minutes, until tender. Drain and run under cold water. When cool enough to handle, scrape the kernels off the cob with a sharp knife. Set aside.

3. In a separate bowl, mix the cornmeal, flour, sugar, baking powder, salt, and baking soda.

4. In the bowl of a stand mixer with the whisk attachment, mix together the egg and buttermilk at medium speed. Replace the whisk with the paddle attachment and add the flour mixture. Mix on medium speed. Fold in the tomatoes and 1 cup corn kernels with a large spatula.

5. Set the prepared pan in the oven until it begins to smoke. Remove and pour in the batter. Bake for about 35 minutes, until golden brown; a toothpick inserted in the center should come out clean. Let the bread cool in the pan for 20 minutes, then remove it and cut it into 8 pieces.

corn off the cob and heirloom tomatoes with grilled onions

This is summer in a bowl: full-flavored heirloom tomatoes, sweet corn, which you can only get in summer, and sweet onions, such as Vidalia, Maui, or Walla Walla.

NOTES ▶ **This is not appropriate for children younger than three years old.**

Serves 8

8 ears fresh, sweet corn

Melted butter (optional)

2 large onions

2 tablespoons extra virgin olive oil, plus more for coating onions

Sea salt and freshly ground black pepper

1 teaspoon fresh thyme leaves

8 heirloom tomatoes, quartered

1. To prepare the corn for grilling, pull the husk back from the cob to remove the silk. Fold the husk back and soak the ears in water for 10 minutes. Grill the ears over medium-hot coals for 15 to 20 minutes, turning occasionally. Remove from the heat and set aside to cool. An alternative method allows you to prepare the corn a day ahead. Bring a large pot of unsalted water to a boil. Remove the husks and silk and boil the corn for 2 minutes. Remove and refresh in cold water and drain. At this point the corn can be wrapped in aluminum foil and refrigerated for a day. To grill, brush with melted butter and place over medium-hot coals for about 3 minutes, turning frequently, until lightly charred.

2. To prepare the onions, preheat the oven to 350°F.

3. Cut the onions in half from top to bottom leaving the root end attached. Arrange the onion halves on a sheet tray, cut side up. Coat evenly with oil, salt, pepper, and thyme. Cover with foil and roast for 30 minutes, until tender and easily pierced. The onions can be roasted up to 1 day in advance. Store them covered with the foil at room temperature.

4. Grill the onions over medium-hot coals until lightly charred, 2 to 4 minutes per side. When the onions are cool, remove the root ends and cut each half into thirds.

5. To serve, mix the tomatoes, corn kernels, and onions in a large bowl. Toss with salt and pepper and the 2 tablespoons oil.

baked beans with apple-smoked bacon

The crunchy bacon crust is reason alone to make this baked bean dish, especially if it's made with apple-smoked bacon, which you can find in most markets.

<table>
<tr><td>NOTES ▶</td><td>**For babies nine to twelve months old, purée the beans in a food processor fitted with a steel blade with enough chicken broth to achieve the desired consistency.**</td></tr>
</table>

Serves 8

2 pounds navy or other white beans, rinsed and picked over

1 pound apple-smoked bacon, cut into thin strips, plus 10 whole strips

½ sweet onion, finely chopped

1 cup pure maple syrup

1 cup dark molasses

2 teaspoons Dijon mustard

1 cup low-sodium chicken broth (optional)

Sea salt and freshly ground black pepper

Dried breadcrumbs

1. Cover the beans with cold water and soak overnight. Rinse, drain, and set aside.

2. In a large ovenproof casserole over medium-high heat, cook the sliced bacon strips for about 3 minutes, until the fat is translucent. Add the onion and cook for about 5 minutes, until it is soft, stirring occasionally with a wooden spoon.

3. Add the beans and coat well with the bacon and onion mixture. Cover with 1 inch of water, cover, and cook over medium-high heat for 1 hour, stirring occasionally.

4. Preheat the oven to 350°F.

5. Add the syrup, molasses, and mustard to the beans and mix well. Place the casserole in the oven, covered, and bake for about 2 hours, until the beans are tender. Check occasionally to make sure the beans aren't dry. Stir in the 1 cup chicken broth if necessary to maintain a creamy consistency. When the beans are tender, remove from the oven and mix, bringing the bacon up from the bottom. Season with salt and pepper.

6. Partially cook the whole bacon strips in a large sauté pan for about 3 minutes, until the fat is translucent. Remove and drain on paper towels. Place the strips on top of the beans and cover with a thin layer of breadcrumbs.

7. Turn the oven up to 400°F. Return the casserole to the oven and bake, uncovered, about 5 minutes, until the breadcrumbs are browned and the beans are bubbling.

8. Serve warm directly out of the casserole.

roasted yukon gold potato slices

Instead of potato salad, I like to serve crunchy roasted Yukon gold potato slices. Choose potatoes equal in size so that the slices make an attractive pattern when you overlap them on the serving dish.

NOTES > Remove a few potato slices before brushing with the vinaigrette and purée with some water to the desired consistency for babies six to nine months old; mash them into bite-size lumps for babies nine months to two years old.

Serves 8

3 pounds medium Yukon gold
potatoes, cut lengthwise
into ½-inch-thick slices
(do not peel)

6 tablespoons extra virgin
olive oil

Sea salt and freshly ground
black pepper

BALSAMIC VINAIGRETTE

1½ tablespoons balsamic
vinegar

6 tablespoons extra virgin
olive oil

1 teaspoon Dijon mustard

Fresh thyme leaves

Fresh rosemary sprigs, for
garnish

1. Preheat the oven to 350°F.

2. Coat the potato slices generously with the oil. Season with salt and pepper.

3. Arrange the slices in a single layer on a sheet pan and cover tightly with aluminum foil. Roast for about 15 minutes. Turn the slices over and roast, uncovered, for 10 to 12 minutes, until golden brown.

4. To prepare the vinaigrette, while the potatoes are roasting, whisk together the vinegar, oil, and mustard.

5. To serve, place the slices in an overlapping pattern on a large platter and brush with the vinaigrette. Sprinkle with thyme leaves and garnish with a couple sprigs of rosemary.

rich chocolate brownies with warm chocolate sauce

I'm a chocoholic. I admit it and this certainly is the proof, although Christine and I have always restricted our boys' access to the tempting stuff.

NOTES ▶ **Restrict chocolate until your baby is over two years old.**

Makes 9 to 12 brownies

BROWNIES

4 ounces unsweetened chocolate, chopped

2 ounces bittersweet chocolate, chopped

1 cup unsalted butter

2 cups sugar

1 teaspoon vanilla extract

4 large eggs

1¼ cups all-purpose flour

1 teaspoon sea salt

½ cup chopped pecans or walnuts

WARM CHOCOLATE SAUCE

1¼ cups heavy whipping cream

13 ounces semisweet chocolate

1. Preheat the oven to 350°F. Line a 9-inch square baking pan with parchment paper.

2. Melt the chocolate and butter until smooth in a heat-proof bowl over a pan of simmering water. Remove from the heat and transfer to the bowl of a stand mixer fitted with the paddle attachment.

3. Add 1 cup of the sugar to the melted chocolate and beat on medium-high speed for five minutes. Beat in the vanilla.

4. Replace the paddle with the whisk and, in a separate mixing bowl, whisk the eggs and remaining 1 cup of sugar on high speed for 2 minutes, until light and fluffy. Switch back to the paddle and, with the mixer on low, slowly add the chocolate mixture to the egg mixture. Gently fold in the flour, salt, and nuts.

5. Turn the batter into the prepared pan. Bake for about 60 minutes. Test by inserting a toothpick into the center of the brownies; it should come out with a light coating of batter. The brownies should be moist.

6. Remove the pan from oven and cool on a rack for about 20 minutes. Remove the brownies from the pan and let cool completely on the rack.

7. While the brownies are cooling, prepare the chocolate sauce. Heat the cream in a heavy-bottomed saucepan and add the chocolate. Remove from the heat and stir until fully blended. Transfer to a serving bowl.

8. Cut the brownie into 2-inch squares; serve the chocolate sauce on the side.

lemon sponge cake with mixed summer berries

This is light, delicious, and a spectacular enough presentation to provide an appropriate finish to a Fourth-of-July buffet. And it's red, white, and blue.

> **NOTES**
>
> **Family members from one year old and up can enjoy this, but be sure to mash the berries for children under three years, since they can present a choking hazard.**

Serves 10 to 12

LEMON SPONGE CAKE

2 tablespoons water

½ teaspoon vanilla extract

1½ teaspoons grated lemon zest

1⅓ cups sifted cake flour

1 cup sugar

6 large eggs, separated

¾ teaspoon cream of tartar

MASCARPONE CREAM

⅓ cup mascarpone

2 cups heavy cream

2 tablespoons confectioners' sugar

BERRIES

1 cup blueberries

1 cup strawberries, trimmed and halved

1 cup blackberries

1 cup raspberries

1. Preheat the oven to 350°F. Line a 10-inch springform pan with parchment paper and lightly grease the sides.

2. To prepare the cake, combine the water, vanilla, and lemon zest, and set aside.

3. In a medium bowl, combine the flour and 3 tablespoons of the sugar.

4. In the bowl of a stand mixer fitted with the whisk attachment, beat the egg yolks and the remaining sugar on high speed until the mixture is thick and forms a ribbon, 5 to 10 minutes. Replace the whisk attachment with the paddle, and, on low speed, add the water-vanilla mixture in a thin stream. Beat on low just until blended, less than a minute.

5. Remove the bowl from the mixer and sift the combined flour and sugar over the mixture but do not blend.

6. In a separate bowl, beat on high the egg whites until they are foamy, add the cream of tartar, and continue beating on high until soft peaks form.

7. Using a large rubber spatula, gently fold one-third of the egg whites into the yolk mixture. Repeat this process two more times until all the egg whites are fully blended in.

8. Turn the batter into the prepared pan. Bake for 30 minutes, until a toothpick inserted in the center of the cake comes out clean.

(continued on page 153)

CONTINUED FROM PAGE 151

9. Cool on a rack for 20 minutes, then remove the cake from the pan and let cool completely.

10. To prepare the mascarpone cream, in the bowl of an electric mixer fitted with the paddle attachment, beat the mascarpone on high until light and fluffy.

11. In a separate bowl, using the mixer's whisk attachment, whip the cream and sugar on high until thick but not holding peaks. Switch back to the paddle attachment and add the mascarpone, mixing on low until fully blended.

12. To prepare the mixed berries, simply combine the berries in a large bowl and set aside.

13. To assemble, slice the cake in half horizontally to make two layers. Place one layer, cut side up on, a serving platter and spread thickly with the mascarpone cream. Cover with the other layer, cut side down, and spoon the mixed berries on top, letting some collect around the bottom. Sift the confectioners' sugar over the berries and cake, and cut into wedges to serve. Alternatively, you can leave the cake whole, cut it into wedges, and serve the mascarpone cream and berries in separate bowls on the side.

Family Feasts

Recommended Reading

Atkinson, Catherine. *Real Food for Baby*. London: Foulsham & Co., Ltd., 2001.

Berman, Christine, M.P.H., R.D. & Jackie Fromer. *Meals Without Squeals: Child Care Feeding Guide & Cookbook*. Palo Alto: Bull Publishing Company, 1997.

Charlton, Carol. *Family Organic Cookbook*. Newton Abbot, UK: Charles & David, 2000.

Coyle, Rena. *Baby Let's Eat*. New York: Workman Publishing Company, 1997.

Hodgman, Ann. *One Bite Won't Kill You*. New York: Houghton Mifflin Company, 1999.

Kalnins, Diana, R.D., C.N.S.D. & Joanne Saab, R.D. *America's Complete Source: Better Baby Food*. Toronto: Robert Rose, Inc., 2001.

Karmel, Annabel. *First Meals*. New York: Dorling Kindersley Publishing, Inc., 1999.

Karmel, Annabel. *The Healthy Baby Meal Planner*. New York: Fireside, 1992.

Kimmel, Martha & David Kimmel, with Suzanne Goldenson. *Mommy Made* and Daddy Too! Home Cooking for a Healthy Baby & Toddler*. New York: Bantam Books, 2000.

Knight, Karin, R.N. & Jeannie Lumley. *The Baby Cookbook: Nutrition, Feeding, and Cooking for Babies Six Months to Two Years of Age*. Revised. New York: William Morrow, 1992.

Lair, Cynthia. *Feeding the Whole Family: Whole Foods Recipes for Babies, Young Children and Their Parents*. Seattle: Moon Smile Press, 1997.

Lewis, Sara. *First Food: Preparing Food for Babies and Toddlers*. Bath, UK: Southwater, 2000.

Null, Shelly. *Healthy Cooking for Kids: Building Blocks of a Lifetime of Cooking.* New York: St. Martin's Griffin, 1999.

Satter, Ellyn. *Child of Mine: Feeding with Love and Good Sense.* 3rd edition. Palo Alto: Bull Publishing Company, 2000.

Stanway, Penny, Dr. *Good Food for Kids.* USA and Canada: Creative Publishing International, Inc., 2000.

Sweet, Robin O. & Thomas A. Bloom, Ph.D. *The Well Fed Baby: Healthy, Delicious Baby Food Recipes That You Can Make at Home.* New York: William Morrow, 2000.

Swinney, Bridget. *Healthy Food for Healthy Kids: A Practical and Tasty Guide to Your Child's Nutrition.* New York: Meadowbrook Press, 1999.

Tamborlane, William V., M.D., editor. *The Yale Guide to Children's Nutrition.* New Haven & London: Yale University Press, 1997.

Tarlov, Janet Mason. *The Everything Baby's First Food Book.* Holbrook, MA: Adams Media Corporation, 2001.

Vann, Lizzie. *Organic Baby & Toddler Cookbook: Easy Recipes for Natural Food.* New York: Dorling Kindersley Publishing, Inc., 2001.

Wiel, Andrew, M.D. *Eating Well for Optimum Health.* New York: Random House, Inc., 2000.

Yaron, Ruth. *Super Baby Food.* 2nd edition, revised. Archibald, PA: F. J. Roberts Publishing, 2000.

Metric Conversions

LIQUID WEIGHT

U.S. Measurement	*Metric Equivalent*
¼ teaspoon	1.23 ml
½ teaspoon	2.5 ml
¾ teaspoon	3.7 ml
1 teaspoon	5 ml
1 dessert spoon	10 ml
1 tablespoon (3 teaspoons)	15 ml
2 tablespoons (1 ounce)	30 ml
¼ cup	60 ml
⅓ cup	80 ml
½ cup	120 ml
⅔ cup	160 ml
¾ cup	180 ml
1 cup (8 ounces)	240 ml
2 cups (1 pint)	480 ml
3 cups	720 ml
4 cups (1 quart)	1 liter
4 quarts (1 gallon)	3¾ liter

DRY WEIGHT

U.S. Measurement	*Metric Equivalent*
¼ ounce	7 grams
⅓ ounce	10 grams
½ ounce	14 grams
1 ounce	28 grams
1½ ounces	42 grams
1¾ ounces	50 grams
2 ounces	57 grams
3 ounces	85 grams
3½ ounces	100 grams
4 ounces (¼ pound)	114 grams
6 ounces	170 grams
8 ounces (½ pound)	227 grams
9 ounces	250 grams
16 ounces (1 pound)	464 grams
1.1 pounds	500 grams
2.2 pounds	1,000 grams

TEMPERATURES

Fahrenheit	*Celsius (Centigrade)*
32°F (water freezes)	0°C
200°F	95°C
212°F (water boils)	100°C
225°F	110°C
250°F	120°C
275°F	135°C
300°F (slow oven)	150°C
325°F	160°C
350°F (moderate oven)	175°C
375°F	190°C
400°F (hot oven)	205°C
425°F	220°C
450°F (very hot oven)	230°C
475°F	245°C
500°F (extremely hot oven)	260°C

LENGTH

U.S. Measurement	*Metric Equivalent*
⅛ inch	3 mm
¼ inch	6 mm
⅜ inch	1 cm
½ inch	12 mm
¾ inch	2 cm
1 inch	2.5 cm
2 inches	5 cm
3 inches	7.5 cm
4 inches	10 cm
5 inches	12.5 cm

APPROXIMATE EQUIVALENTS

1 kilo is slightly more than 2 pounds

1 liter is slightly more than 1 quart

1 deciliter is slightly less than ½ cup

1 meter is slightly over 3 feet

1 centiliter is approximately 2 teaspoons

1 centimeter is approximately ⅜ inch

Index

A

Acorn Squash Purée, Roasted, 14
Allergies, 3–4
Almond Cake, Orange, 120
Apples
    Apple Apricot Compote, 93
    Apple Ginger Pie with Vanilla
        Sauce and Spiced Cream,
        105–7
    Brown Rice with Hazelnut
        and Apple Purée, 50
    caramelizing, 8
    Green Salad with
        Pomegranate, Apples,
        Pecans, and Oranges,
        112–13
    Parsnips, Apples, and Sweet
        Onions, 31
Apricots
    Apple Apricot Compote, 93
    Braised Pork with Apricots
        and Onions, 86
Artichokes with Extra Virgin
    Olive Oil, 66
Asparagus and Eight-Minute Egg
    with Champagne
    Vinaigrette, 126
Avocado with Onion and
    Cilantro, 67

B

Baby Back Pork Ribs in a Sweet
    Marinade, 144–45
Bacon
    Baked Beans with Apple-
        Smoked Bacon, 147

Fresh Peas, Onions, and
    Apple-Smoked Bacon, 73
Green, Brown, and Pink
    Lentils with Apple-Smoked
    Bacon, 48
String Beans with Garlic
    Croutons and Bacon, 101
White Beans and Parsley, 75
Balsamic Vinaigrette, 148
Bananas
    Banana Peach Compote, 44
    Banana Purée with Ground
        Hazelnuts, 60
    Black Beans and Banana with
        Crème Fraîche, 37
Beans
    Baked Beans with Apple-
        Smoked Bacon, 147
    Black Beans and Banana with
        Crème Fraîche, 37
    Garbanzo Bean Casserole, 74
    Green Beans and Wax Beans, 19
    String Beans with Garlic
        Croutons and Bacon, 101
    White Beans and Parsley, 75
Beef
    Classic Beef Stew, 84
    Salt-Crusted Beef Rib Roast,
        114
Beets
    Roasted Beet and Orange
        Juice Purée, 68
    Roasted Large-Dice Root
        Vegetables, 119
Berries, Mixed Summer, Lemon
    Sponge Cake with, 151–53
Biscuits, 88

Blanching, 7
Blenders, 9
Braising, 8
Bran Muffins with Currants,
    Dried Cranberries, and
    Pecans, 89
Breads
    Biscuits, 88
    Bran Muffins with Currants,
        Dried Cranberries, and
        Pecans, 89
    Cheddar Cheese Muffins, 57
    Corn and Tomato Bread, 145
    Focaccia, 42–43
    Popovers, 115
    Rosemary Bread Sticks, 22–23
Broccoli
    Broccoli and Cauliflower
        Purée, 27
    Sautéed Broccoli Purée, 26
Brownies, Rich Chocolate, with
    Warm Chocolate Sauce, 150
Brussels Sprouts, Sweet Onion,
    and Nutmeg, 70
Butter
    Cilantro Butter, 80
    concerns about, 23
Butternut Squash Soup with
    Wild Mushroom Crouton,
    111–12

C

Cabbage, Napa or Savoy, with
    Lemon, 71
Cakes
    Flourless Chocolate Hazelnut
        Cake, 138–39

Cakes, *continued*
    Lemon Sponge Cake with
        Mixed Summer Berries,
        151–53
    Orange Almond Cake with
        Orange Syrup and Crème
        Fraîche, 120
Caramel Cranberry Sauce, 102
Caramelizing, 8
Carrots
    Carrot Purée with Lemon, 28
    Carrot with Chicken Broth
        Purée, 16
    Classic Beef Stew, 84
    Couscous with Cauliflower
        and Carrots, 39
    Green or Brown Lentil
        with Carrot and Shallot
        Purée, 20
    Lamb Stew with Carrots and
        Prunes, 85
    Roasted Large-Dice Root
        Vegetables, 119
    Wild Rice Risotto with
        Carrots and Celery, 76
    Wild Rice with Mushrooms
        and Onions, 78
Cauliflower
    Broccoli and Cauliflower
        Purée, 27
    Couscous with Cauliflower
        and Carrots, 39
Celery root
    Celery Root and Fresh Basil
        Purée, 30
    Roasted Large-Dice Root
        Vegetables, 119
Champagne Vinaigrette, 112–13,
    126
Cheese
    Cheddar Cheese Muffins, 57
    Grits and Spinach with
        California Cheddar, 51
    Mascarpone Cream, 151, 153
    Pumpkin Risotto Stuffing,
        99–100
    Sweet Potato Risotto, 43
    Tomato and Basil Risotto, 77
    Wild Rice with Mushrooms
        and Onions, 78
Chicken
    Barbecue Chicken in a Spicy
        Marinade, 142
    Chicken Pot Pie, 52–54

    Matzo Ball Soup, 131
Chocolate
    Chocolate Chip Shortbread, 90
    Flourless Chocolate Hazelnut
        Cake, 138–39
    Rich Chocolate Brownies with
        Warm Chocolate Sauce, 150
Choking, 4
Christmas, 108–20
Cilantro Butter, 80
Compotes
    Apple Apricot Compote, 93
    Banana Peach Compote, 44
    Peach Honey Compote with
        Lemon or Lime, 61
    Plum Honey Compote, 62
Cookies
    Chocolate Chip Shortbread, 90
    Orange Sable Cookies, 91
    Rich Chocolate Brownies with
        Warm Chocolate Sauce, 150
Corn
    Corn and Tomato Bread, 145
    Corn off the Cob and
        Heirloom Tomatoes with
        Grilled Onions, 146
    Couscous with Corn and Pea
        Purée, 18
    Grilled Lobster, Corn, and
        Red Pepper, 80–82
Couscous
    Couscous with Cauliflower
        and Carrots, 39
    Couscous with Corn and Pea
        Purée, 18
    Salmon with Couscous and
        Roasted Green Onions, 40
Cranberries
    Bran Muffins with Currants,
        Dried Cranberries, and
        Pecans, 89
    Caramel Cranberry Sauce,
        102
Cream, Spiced, 107
Crème Caramel, 59–60
Currants, Bran Muffins with
    Dried Cranberries, Pecans,
    and, 89

D
Deglazing, 8
Dessert, attitude toward, 88
Dutch ovens, 11

E
Easter, 122–28
Eggs
    Asparagus and Eight-Minute
        Egg with Champagne
        Vinaigrette, 126
    Crème Caramel, 59–60
Equipment, 9–11

F
Fat, 23
Fish
    Salmon with Couscous and
        Roasted Green Onions, 40
    Tuna with Baby Spinach and
        Tomatoes, 83
    White Fish and Basil in
        Mashed Potatoes, 55
Flourless Chocolate Hazelnut
    Cake, 138–39
Focaccia, 42–43
Food processors, 9
Fourth of July, 140–53
Freezing, 8–9

G
Garbanzo Bean Casserole, 74
Green beans
    Green Beans and Wax Beans, 19
    String Beans with Garlic
        Croutons and Bacon, 101
Green Salad with Pomegranate,
    Apples, Pecans, and
    Oranges, 112–13
Grits and Spinach with
    California Cheddar, 51

H
Ham, Fresh Sweet Peas and, 34
Hazelnuts
    Banana Purée with Ground
        Hazelnuts, 60
    Brown Rice with Hazelnut
        and Apple Purée, 50
    Flourless Chocolate Hazelnut
        Cake, 138–39
Honey
    Peach Honey Compote with
        Lemon or Lime, 61
    Plum Honey Compote, 62

I
Ice cube trays, 11

feeding baby

L

Lactose intolerance, 4
Lamb
  Lamb Stew with Carrots and
    Prunes, 85
  Roasted Leg of Lamb with
    Spring Vegetables and
    Shiitake Mushrooms,
    123–24
Leek and Potato Purée, 32
Lemon Sponge Cake with Mixed
  Summer Berries, 151–53
Lentils
  Green, Brown, and Pink
    Lentils with Apple-Smoked
    Bacon, 48
  Green or Brown Lentil
    with Carrot and Shallot
    Purée, 20
  Pink Lentil and Peach Purée, 21
Lobster, Corn, and Red Pepper,
  Grilled, 80–82

M

Mascarpone Cream, 151, 153
Matzo Ball Soup, 131
Meal times
  in Europe, 77
  scheduled, 16
Milk, 4
Mixers, 9–10
Muffins
  Bran Muffins with Currants,
    Dried Cranberries, and
    Pecans, 89
  Cheddar Cheese Muffins, 57
Mushrooms
  Butternut Squash Soup with
    Wild Mushroom Crouton,
    111–12
  Pumpkin Risotto Stuffing,
    99–100
  Roasted Leg of Lamb with
    Spring Vegetables and
    Shiitake Mushrooms,
    123–24
  Wild Rice with Mushrooms
    and Onions, 78

N

Napa or Savoy Cabbage with
  Lemon, 71

O

Olive oil, 18
Onions
  Braised Pork with Apricots
    and Onions, 86
  caramelizing, 8
  Corn off the Cob and
    Heirloom Tomatoes with
    Grilled Onions, 146
  Creamed Cipollini Onions
    and Spinach, 117
  Fresh Peas, Onions, and
    Apple-Smoked Bacon, 73
  Roasted Large-Dice Root
    Vegetables, 119
  Salmon with Couscous and
    Roasted Green Onions, 40
  Wild Rice with Mushrooms
    and Onions, 78
Oranges
  Green Salad with
    Pomegranate, Apples,
    Pecans, and Oranges,
    112–13
  Orange Almond Cake with
    Orange Syrup and Crème
    Fraîche, 120
  Orange Sable Cookies, 91
  Roasted Beet and Orange
    Juice Purée, 68
Organic produce, 18

P

Panna Cotta with Balsamic
  Marinated Strawberries,
  128
Parchment paper, 11
Parsnips
  Parsnips, Apples, and Sweet
    Onions, 31
  Roasted Large-Dice Root
    Vegetables, 119
Passover, 129–39
Peaches
  Banana Peach Compote, 44
  Peach Honey Compote with
    Lemon or Lime, 61
  Pink Lentil and Peach Purée, 21
Pears, Turnips, and Parsley, 35
Peas
  Couscous with Corn and Pea
    Purée, 18
  Fresh Peas, Onions, and
    Apple-Smoked Bacon, 73

Fresh Pea with Mint Purée, 17
  Fresh Sweet Peas and Ham, 34
Pecans
  Bran Muffins with Currants,
    Dried Cranberries, and
    Pecans, 89
  Caramelized Pecans, 112–13
  Green Salad with
    Pomegranate, Apples,
    Pecans, and Oranges,
    112–13
Picky eaters, 67
Pies
  Apple Ginger Pie with Vanilla
    Sauce and Spiced Cream,
    105–7
  Chicken Pot Pie, 52–54
Plum Honey Compote, 62
Pomegranate, Green Salad with
  Apples, Pecans, Oranges,
  and, 112–13
Popovers, 115
Pork. *See also* Bacon
  Baby Back Pork Ribs in a
    Sweet Marinade, 144–45
  Braised Pork with Apricots
    and Onions, 86
  Fresh Sweet Peas and Ham, 34
Potatoes
  Classic Beef Stew, 84
  Potato and Leek Purée, 32
  Roasted Herbed New
    Potatoes, 125
  Roasted Yukon Gold Potato
    Slices, 148
  Super Mashed Potatoes, 104
  White Fish and Basil in
    Mashed Potatoes, 55
Potato ricers, 10
Pot Pie, Chicken, 52–54
Protein, 54
Prunes, Lamb Stew with Carrots
  and, 85
Pudding, Rice, 63
Pumpkin Risotto Stuffing,
  99–100

R

Refreshing, 7
Reheating, 8–9
Restaurants, 62–63
Rice. *See also* Wild rice
  Brown Rice with Hazelnut
    and Apple Purée, 50

Rice, *continued*
  Pumpkin Risotto Stuffing,
    99–100
  Rice Pudding, 63
  Shrimp and Scallop Risotto, 79
  Sweet Potato Risotto, 43
  Tomato and Basil Risotto, 77
Rosemary Bread Sticks, 22–23

S
Safety, 3–4, 8–9
Salad, Green, with Pomegranate,
    Apples, Pecans, and
    Oranges, 112–13
Salmon with Couscous and
    Roasted Green Onions, 40
Salt, 4–5, 18
Salt-Crusted Beef Rib Roast, 114
Sauces
  Caramel Cranberry Sauce, 102
  Vanilla Sauce, 106
  Warm Chocolate Sauce, 150
Scallop and Shrimp Risotto, 79
Shortbread, Chocolate Chip, 90
Shrimp and Scallop Risotto, 79
Sieves, 10
Solid food, introducing, 13, 23
Soups
  Butternut Squash Soup with
    Wild Mushroom Crouton,
    111–12
  Matzo Ball Soup, 131
Spiced Cream, 107
Spinach
  Creamed Cipollini Onions
    and Spinach, 117
  Creamed Spinach, 33
  Grits and Spinach with
    California Cheddar, 51
  Spinach with Pine Nuts, 136

Tuna with Baby Spinach and
    Tomatoes, 83
Spoons, wooden, 10
Squash
  Butternut Squash Soup with
    Wild Mushroom Crouton,
    111–12
  Roasted Acorn Squash
    Purée, 14
Stand mixers, 9
Steamers, 10
Stews
  Classic Beef Stew, 84
  Lamb Stew with Carrots and
    Prunes, 85
Stick blenders, 9
Strainers, 10
Strawberries
  Lemon Sponge Cake with
    Mixed Summer Berries,
    151–53
  Panna Cotta with Balsamic
    Marinated Strawberries,
    128
String Beans with Garlic
    Croutons and Bacon, 101
Stuffing, Pumpkin Risotto,
    99–100
Super Mashed Potatoes, 104
Sweet Potato Risotto, 43

T
Techniques, 7–9
Thanksgiving, 96–107
Thawing, 8–9
Tomatoes
  Corn and Tomato Bread, 145
  Corn off the Cob and
    Heirloom Tomatoes with
    Grilled Onions, 146

Tomato and Basil Risotto, 77
Tuna with Baby Spinach and
    Tomatoes, 83
Traveling, 61
Tuna with Baby Spinach and
    Tomatoes, 83
Turkey, Roasted Young, with
    Pumpkin Risotto Stuffing,
    99–100
Turnips
  Mashed Turnips, 116
  Turnips, Pears, and Parsley, 35

V
Vanilla Sauce, 106
Veal Shank, Braised, with Spring
    Vegetables, 132–34
Vegetables. *See also individual
    vegetables*
  blanching, 7
  Roasted Large-Dice Root
    Vegetables, 119
Vinaigrettes
  Balsamic Vinaigrette, 148
  Champagne Vinaigrette,
    112–13, 126

W
White Fish and Basil in Mashed
    Potatoes, 55
Wild rice
  Wild Rice Risotto with
    Carrots and Celery, 76
  Wild Rice with Mushrooms
    and Onions, 78

feeding baby